Natural Religion

in

American Literature

Arnold Smithline

COLLEGE & UNIVERSITY PRESS · *Publishers*

NEW HAVEN, CONN.

PS
166
.54

For

Leona, Helene, and Jerry

Acknowledgments

I am indebted to Professor Gay Wilson Allen of New York University for his wise guidance and assistance as the work progressed. He made many valuable suggestions, and I relied extensively on his vast knowledge of Whitman and the Transcendentalists. Professors Oscar Cargill and Nelson F. Adkins read the manuscript in its various stages of completion and made helpful comments and suggestions. I should also mention Professor Roderick Marshall of Brooklyn College in my list of acknowledgments. It was in his course, Foreign Influences on American Literature, that the idea of the book was probably first conceived, and whose influence appears throughout, especially in the section dealing with Emerson and Oriental thought.

Finally, I would like to thank my wife for her unflagging encouragement and support, and her immeasurable aid in preparing the manuscript and index.

Permission to quote from John Steinbeck's *Grapes of Wrath* has been granted by Viking Press; from Walter Van Tilburg Clark's *Ox-Bow Incident* by Random House; and from Wallace Stevens' "Sunday Morning" by Alfred A. Knopf.

Contents

Introduction

In 1721 Cotton Mather wrote the *Christian Philosopher,* a book anticipating deism, in that it extolled the order and harmony in nature which it referred to as the "second revelation of God." From that time, American literature has continually concerned itself with developing and expanding this concept in an effort to evolve a "religion" which would be an expression of the national consciousness. The inherited religion of the Puritans began to lose ground at the turn of the eighteenth century, and in its place deism developed. Mather's book represents probably the earliest expression in any consistent form of deistic thought in America. In viewing nature as the "second revelation," it wedged an opening in the armor of Puritan theology which was widened considerably by the attacks on traditional Christianity by the militant deists, Ethan Allen and Tom Paine. *Reason, The Only Oracle of Man* (1784) and *The Age of Reason* (1792) rejected supernatural revelation as absurd and repugnant to reason and common sense. Thus, natural religion in American literature was born.

The deists believed in a God who created the universe according to perfect laws by which it continued to operate. These perfect and universal laws could be understood by man through reason alone. Man, they believed, was naturally good and needed no divine grace in order to ensure his salvation. Moral laws were conceived as archetypal and derivable from the order and harmony of nature itself. No supernaturally ordained moral code was necessary because these laws were "imprinted" within man by the Deity; thus, by heeding the dictates of his own conscience, the individual would be following the moral law.

Deism originated in England in the late seventeenth and early eighteenth centuries. The growth of deistic thought is generally attributed to the rise of scientific inquiry, the physics of Newton in which the universe was seen to operate according to mechanistic laws, and the philosophy of John Locke who incorporated Newton's discoveries placing man in a new relation with nature. Locke himself was not fully aware of the implications his thought held for religion; for if nature were such a supreme source of truth, how much need was there for Christian revelation? Actually, the Church in trying to assimilate the philosophy of reason into the Christian doctrine was as much the cause of the rise of deism as was the scientific philosophy. "The very theologians who had done most to encourage the free play of reason began to fulminate against the logical consequence of their own work."[1] Toland, in *Christianity Not Mysterious* (1696) had gone beyond the traditional bounds and made too strong a case for rationalism. The controversy it gave rise to served as a warning to others. The law against heresy was enacted in 1697, and "Englishmen who believed, a century in advance of Thomas Paine, what he boldly proclaims in the *Age of Reason* (1792) had to express their views with great circumspection."[2]

However, it remained for Lord Herbert of Cherbury to give more formal definition to the implications the new science and philosophy held for religion. Familiarly cited as "the father of deism," Lord Herbert in *De Veritate,* (1624) states his aim to be the discovery of an infallible method by which Truth may be distinguished from Error.[3] Cherbury is really an early student of comparative religion, for he sought to find a "common denominator" among the multiplicity of religions. He was not so much concerned with reducing the Christian creed to the minimum possible number of fundamentals as were Jeremy Taylor and the current school of rational theologians; "he goes beyond Christianity itself, and tries to formulate a belief which shall command the universal assent of all men."[4] Herbert's method follows that of the age in which he lived; that is, all difficulties were "referred to an inner tribunal presided over by 'Reason, Nature,' or 'Truths of first inscription.'"[5] Proceeding in this manner, Herbert discovers the principle of certainty in the "natural instincts," the "common notions." "Whatsoever is vouched for by the notions commonly inscribed upon the minds of men as such, whatsoever is received by universal consent, that, and that only, is Truth."[6] And truth is arrived at not by analyzing all theological systems and religious doctrines, but by the inner faculty:

> Now we derive this universal consent not only from laws, religions, philosophies, and the written remains of all kinds of authors, but we claim further that there are certain faculties innate in us by means of which these truths are vouched for.[7]

All that is necessary then, is to draw upon the inner faculty and give it free rein; we fall into error only by the disuse of the touchstone with which nature has supplied us.

> For I boldly say that there have been and are now, men, Churches and schools, stuffed with *bagatelles,* which have introduced into succeeding centuries impostures and fables ... having no other foundation than true-seeming stories, or some rude or impertinent reasoning; a thing which would never have happened if my method had been followed.
>
> The common notions are the principles against which it is not permissible to dispute, or indeed they are that part of science which nature has given us, according to her first intention. It is in these notions, as I have many times said, that we see shining a gleam of the divine wisdom, when we separate them from the impurity of opinions.[8]

Of course, the question remains, by what criterion can Lord Herbert infallibly distinguish a "common notion" from an "impure opinion"? From our present vantage point the reply would be, "a common notion" was a kind which, to a man of his type of culture and at his particular stage of civilization, seemed "indisputably 'true' because it satisfied his deepest needs. An impure opinion was one which disappointed or thwarted those particular needs."[9]

In deriving a means of arriving at his list of common notions, however, Herbert is quite precise. We must seek the required religious formulation in two ways—first by the study of comparative religion:

> Religion is a common notion, for there has never been a century nor any nation without religion. We must therefore see what universal consent has brought to light in religion, and compare all that we find on this subject, so as to receive as common notions all things which are recognizably present and constant in the true religion.[10]

And secondly, one may adhere to the dictates of the inner voice, a much more direct and less laborious way:

> Nay, if you desire a more expeditious method, I will give it to you: Retire into yourself and enter into your own faculties; you will find there God, virtue and the other universal and eternal truths.[11]

The discovery of these fundamental, universal religious concepts is necessary since only in this way can we be defended against priestcraft, a sworn enemy of Lord Herbert. The Church is wrong in claiming to be infallible in religious doctrine, and it is most insidious in proclaiming "that human reason is blind, that it ought to yield to Faith; . . . that no man should trust so far to the resources of his intelligence as to dare to examine the power and authority of Prelates, and of those who declare the word of God."[12] It is for these reasons that we must establish preambles and foundations of religion by the light of the universal wisdom.

Cherbury then gives his list of common notions, which he feels, after studying all the known religions and consulting his own heart, to be the essence of all religious belief. He formulates them under five headings.

1. *That there is a Supreme Power.* "We call then God, him [sic] who has received so many names amongst all sorts of nations." He is eternal, sovereignly good, the creator of all things, and he is the "milieu" in which all things subsist.

2. *That this Sovereign Power must be worshiped.* The means may vary—but common consent ordains this worship. Since some religious cult of one kind or another is found everywhere, Herbert postulates this as a fundamental principle, and concludes from it that religion is the distinguishing characteristic of mankind. "Those who appear to be atheists are generally those who, disgusted at the horrible things attributed to God by deluded men, prefer believing in no God to believing in this one."[13] If, on the other hand, the divine attributes were rightly conceived, these people would be more inclined to believe than not.

3. *That the good ordering or disposition of the faculties of man constitutes the principal or best part of divine worship, and that this has always been believed.* Men may have disputed about ceremonies, but about the necessity for good conduct there has always been agreement. Piety and holiness of life are forms of worship, for they naturally draw us toward a love of God. We have to contend with our bodily nature, but nature has instilled in us a knowledge of virtue, so that our soul can be detached from earthly things, and dwell constantly in inner joy and serenity.

4. *That all vices and crimes should be expiated and effaced by repentance.*

5. *That there are rewards and punishments after this life.* Concluding his list, Cherbury says that the common notions which recognize a sovereign Creator of all things, which bid us honor him, lead pure lives, repent of our sins, and expect reward or punishment after death, "come from God, and are imprinted in the whole human race."[14] Those which assume the existence of many gods, which permit sin to remain unexpiated, and which are doubtful as to the immortality of the soul, are not common notions nor truths.[15]

Herbert has, in effect, defined some of the principal ideas which were later to form the basis of "natural religion." Basil Willey gives a good definition of the movement:

This is the archetypal religion imprinted in all men in all times and places, of which all particular religious cults are derivatives. Ceremonies and usages superimposed on these primary common notions may have their use in religion, but they are not essential. The simple articles of natural religion, which underlie all particular rites and sacraments, contain all that is "necessary for salvation," and so may be used as the basis for religious "comprehension."[16]

Although Herbert is not primarily concerned with "Revelation" in *De Veritate,* his few remarks and reflections on the subject are important because they show how rationalism dealt with this doctrine. "That any truth could be 'given' by sheer force of supernatural authority, so that it must be believed without being understood, was a proposition which became less and less acceptable to most minds as the century proceeded."[17] The notion of revelation was, however, too deeply imbedded in traditional thought to be dealt a death blow at once; it needed to be explained away. For instance, it could be identified with the way the common notions themselves are implanted in our minds. Thus, for Locke, "Reason" became "natural revelation." Herbert retained the original term, but altered its meaning entirely. "The revelation to be genuine, must be made to *oneself;* what is 'revealed' on someone else's authority is only story or tradition."[18] This was precisely the argument Paine later used in his devastating attack on Christian revelation. In addition, Herbert had speculated that the recipient of a revelation should be able to subscribe to its authenticity by some experience of a "particular movement of God" toward him. He sums up his views, practically tossing out supernaturalism and foreshadowing the transcendentalists:

> Every divine and happy sentiment that we feel within our conscience is a revelation, although properly speaking there are no other revelations than those which the inner sense knows to be above the ordinary providence of things.[19]

Another English source of American deism was Anthony Ashley Cooper, Third Earl of Shaftesbury. He wrote a series of essays which were collected and published in 1711 under the familiar title, *Characteristics of Men, Manners, Opinions, and*

Times.[20] Shaftesbury's religious and theological ideas are, in the main, an inheritance from the rationalist movement of the seventeenth century. "There was nothing new in his worship of nature as the sole and perfect manifestation of the Deity, but he managed to give the common belief a fuller and more seductive expression than it had received before."[21] His "poetic ecstasies" over universal beauty and harmony led Montesquieu to call him one of the four great poets of the world. "Pope declared that Shaftesbury did more to weaken the cause of the old religion than all the other deists combined.[22] Here is an example of Shaftesbury's glorification of the order and harmony in nature:

> O glorious Nature! supremely fair and sovereignly good! all-loving and all-lovely, all divine! whose looks are so becoming and of such infinite grace; whose study brings such wisdom and whose contemplation such delight; whose every single work an ampler scene, and is a nobler spectacle than all which ever art presented! O mighty Nature! wise substitute of Providence! impowered creatress! O thou impowering Deity, supreme creator! Thee I invoke and thee alone adore.... I sing of Nature's order in created beings, and celebrate the beauties which resolve in thee, the source and principle of all beauty and perfection....
>
> Yet since by thee, O sovereign mind! I have been formed such as I am, intelligent and rational, since the peculiar dignity of my nature is to know and contemplate thee, permit that with due freedom I exert those faculties with which thou hast adorned me ... be thou my assistant, and guide me in this pursuit whilst I venture thus to tread the labyrinth of wide Nature and endeavor to trace thee in thy works.[23]

It was not only Shaftesbury's unrestrained rationalism that alarmed the clergy, but his use of ridicule as a standard of truth in all matters of religious, as well as secular, dispute. "It was this part of his teaching, more than any other, that eventually provoked the episcopal thunders of Warburton and made his name anathema to the pious; for, rightly or wrongly, he was held largely responsible for the ribald satire of the miracle and mysteries of Christianity which became the sport of freethinkers from Collins to Paine."[24]

Another important aspect of Shaftesbury's thought is the system of ethics he formulated upon the foundation of his natural theology. He believed that man possesses an innate moral sense which can be developed and perfected as any other physical attribute. Therefore the Bible is not needed as a source of morality, since it cannot tell man what he can know by natural means. Shaftesbury is significant in the history of natural religion because "he was among the English pioneers in the endeavor to free morality from the control of dogmatic religion and priestcraft and to establish it upon the basis of an independent science."[25]

> Taking direct issue with his preceptor, Locke, who denied the existence of innate ideas, he held that man is endowed with a moral intuition which is independent of all knowledge, even a knowledge of God, and which distinguishes between vice and virtue as naturally and infallibly as the ear distinguishes between harmony and discord.[26]

This innate moral sense corresponds to the instincts which nature implanted in all animals. Since it functions very much like any of our physical senses, Shaftesbury calls it the moral sense (a term widely used by Emerson and the transcendentalists). While he did not intend to exclude reason from a part in the act of moral judgment, Shaftesbury usually speaks of this moral faculty as a mere impulse, and was never able, apparently, to make a satisfactory adjustment between the intellectual and emotional elements involved. He does say, however, that the moral sense, "though a natural endowment, requires education and training." For without proper exercise it becomes weak and inoperative. The function of reason, then, was to educate the moral faculty. At this point Shaftesbury makes his famous analogy between ethics and esthetics. Men pride themselves, he says, on being connoisseurs of music, painting, and statuary. They pride themselves on their discerning taste in all the fine arts. But they should be taught that there is also a "taste" in morality, and that a fine moral judgment is an esthetic taste extended to the highest level of beauty, the beauty of sentiments and ideas. Only those people who achieve this ability and refinement in esthetics can be called true and virtuous:

> The taste of Beauty and the relish of what is decent, just, and amiable, perfects the character of the Gentleman and the Philosopher. And the study of such a taste or relish will, as we suppose, be ever the great employment and concern of him who covets as well to be wise and good, as agreeable and polite.[27]

Shaftesbury believed that the recognition of virtue leads to the practice of it. In his reflections on morality Shaftesbury makes his strongest attacks on the Church. He feels that the orthodox belief in rewards and punishments in the after life is pernicious. "To do good upon such terms—to be bribed and terrified into decent behavior—is not living the virtuous life."[28] By thus basing morality on fear and bribery, the Church has perverted the true practice of virtue. Following Spinoza, Shaftesbury asserted that virtue is pursued for its own merit. Nature directs the path to goodness, and to be virtuous a man needs only to obey his natural instinct. Just as one observes the beauty in nature, or in art, and sets it off from the discordant and ugly, "so the moral instinct prefers virtue to vice." Goodness, then, is natural to man, vice occurs only when the self is out of harmony with the divine order of the universe. Therefore, moral rewards and punishments are not by supernatural decree but by nature's making. The virtuous, or those who live according to nature, are happy and the vicious make their own hell. Shaftesbury, however, frankly admits that his philosophy is not for the vulgar masses, but is intended for people of culture and refinement, whom he calls the "virtuosos."

The American deists, in general, followed closely the basic concepts advocated by Herbert of Cherbury and Shaftesbury. However, Ethan Allen and Tom Paine seem to reject items four and five of Cherbury's list of common notions—future rewards and punishments, repentance of sins. These, as has been observed, were also rejected by Shaftesbury.

Allen and Paine were more militant than Franklin and Jeffer-

son and other American deists in their attack upon the supernatural authority of the Bible. Allen claimed that "natural
religion was prior to revealed religion," thereby relegating the
Bible to an inferior position in comparison with the primacy of
the truths of nature. Paine condemned the Bible as an "evil"
book disruptive of morality. He attacked its gross excesses, and
its supernatural claims, he felt, were an affront to reason and
common sense. Jefferson's view was less extreme, for he saw
in the Bible great ethical truths which he abstracted, casting
out all passages concerned with miracles and mysteries.

Natural religion, however, changed in form and expression
as American thought and literature developed. But the basic
assumption that man is naturally moral and religiously self-
sufficient was a common notion held by the nineteenth-century
exponents of natural religion, the transcendentalists. What
changed for the most part was the epistemology. The transcendentalists renounced reason but not the fundamental ideas
of deism. They renounced the rationalism used by the Unitarian
theologians as a shallow and inadequate means to divine truths.
According to the transcendantalists, the truths of the soul could
best be reached by instinct and intuition. The fleeting glimpses
of divinity were infinitely superior to the beaten paths of logic
and definition. The transcendentalists, like the deists, were openly hostile to Christian revelation and, for that matter, any
revealed religion. Each man, they believed, is divine, and no
particular creed has exclusive possession of ultimate spiritual
truth. What they accomplished, as far as natural religion was
concerned, was to add an emotional and mystical quality to the
basic beliefs of the deists. Philosophically, this was done through
their concept of monism: they discarded Lockian epistemology,
which teaches that all knowledge comes through the senses. For
the transcendentalists there was an occult relationship between
the mind and the things it observed in nature. Indeed, mind and
matter, or spirit and matter, were one and the same entity.
Emerson said that a natural fact was a symbol of spiritual fact;
and that physical law had its corresponding expression in
moral law.

Whitman signals the culmination of natural religion in nine-teenth-century American literature. He absorbed, consciously or unconsciously, deistic and transcendental ideas and went beyond them. Man not only became for Whitman "part and parcel" of the Oversoul, but was drawn into the life and cosmic process of the whole creation itself. In addition, he wedded natural religion to basic democratic concepts, and thus envisioned a future perfection in which American spiritual democracy would fulfill the age-old ideal of universal brotherhood.

Of the numerous studies of American literature by scholars and historians, few discuss the continuity of the basic ideas and assumptions that are inherent in the term "natural religion." Actually, natural religion, in less comprehensive form, appears in the works of later writers such as, Frank Norris, Theodore Dreiser, and John Steinbeck. Moreover, natural religion continues to be a vital part of the American literary tradition. The various labels assigned to the different periods in that tradition— deism, transcendentalism, naturalism and primitivism—while ac-curate in themselves, tend to blur certain basic similarities.

Randall Stewart in *American Literature and Christian Doctrine* (1958) asserts that the Christian doctrine of Origi-nal Sin is what enobles and best expresses American ex-perience, and is sanctioned by our greatest writers. This position, however, does not square with the facts. There are too many figures in our literature who vigorously oppose this view to give it any general credence. In *American Renaissance*, F. O. Matthiessen has pointed out "two streams" in our literature: the optimistic and more glowing one derived from Emerson and Whitman which stresses the natural goodness of man and his perfectibility; and the darker, more pessimistic one stemming from Hawthorne and James and continuing to Eliot and Faulk-ner, which stresses man's imperfectibility. The latter trend in our literature has drawn the greater amount of scholarly and critical attention in recent years, much to the neglect, and in many cases misrepresentation of the more optimistic tradition. This study attempts to redress this imbalance.

Several historical forces were responsible for the rise of

natural religion: (a) science, (b) the higher criticism of the Bible, and (c) the pragmatic individualism of the American character itself. I shall not be concerned, however, with the sources of natural religion throughout its long development, but shall trace its course through American literature as expressed in the writings of representative figures from Ethan Allen to Walt Whitman.

Natural Religion in American Literature

CHAPTER ONE

Ethan Allen

With the writing of Cotton Mather's *Christian Philosopher,* natural religion made its first appearance in American literature. The motivating force behind the book was the growing Antinomian reaction against the Puritans. The Antinomians asserted that faith alone was all that was necessary to insure one's salvation, and therefore regarded the moral law as unimportant or even unnecessary. This idea angered the Puritan magistrates and led Mather and other leading divines to work out a theological compromise. They thought they ably performed this task not only by taking into account God's transcendence and omnipotence, but equally by stressing His presence in the soul of man and in the creation. The latter concept was in reference to the Antinomian claim of the supremacy of the inner awareness of God's presence. Thus by straddling both concepts, they enunciated the doctrine of two revelations: God's revelation to man in the Bible, and God's revelation to man in Nature.

Mather's *Christian Philosopher,* written in 1721 when orthodoxy was on the wane in New England, glorified the second revelation in both scientific and poetic terms. Mather's method was to show systematically that the creation reflected the design and order of the Creator. He began with a scientific descrip-

23

tion of the planets and stars, working down to the earth with its fauna and flora. Interspersed throughout were descriptive passages where Mather's prose grows rhapsodic and poetic. These ideas expressed in Mather's book proved to be the seed from which developed a line of religious thought which stressed the second revelation, and grew increasingly doubtful of the first, the divine truth of the Scriptures themselves. The growing rationalism of the eighteenth century seized upon this idea and issued a series of vigorous attacks upon virtually all tenets of historical Christianity.

One of these early deistic attacks was Ethan Allen's *Reason, The Only Oracle of Man*. Allen, a Vermont military leader during the Revolutionary War, tells us in the introduction that he was eager to express in writing certain religious convictions that he had begun to formulate earlier in his life. There is still a question how much of the book represents Allen's own ideas and what portion are those of his collaborator, Dr. Thomas Young. Morais gives the following account of the authorship of the book:

> During his youth the future leader of the Green Mountain boys came into contact with an English physician, Thomas Young, who probably acquainted him with Blount and other deistic writers. It is believed that Allen and Young at first agreed to write a free-thinking work together, but later decided that the one who outlived the other was to publish the book. Since Allen survived Young, he inherited the latter's notes.[1]

As the title indicates, Allen rejects all elements of Christianity repugnant to reason and common sense. By thus making a rational and honest inquiry into the nature of God and of religious belief, Allen believed much superstition could be eliminated from religion, a theme which Paine was to seize upon later and enunciate more effectively.

> It is nevertheless to be regretted, that the bulk of mankind, even in those nations which are celebrated for learning and wisdom, are still carried down the torrent of superstition, and entertain very unworthy apprehensions of the Being, Perfection, Creation, and Providence of God. . . . to endeavor

to reclaim mankind from their ignorance and delusion, by
enlightening their minds in those great and sublime truths
concerning God and his Providence, and their obligations
to moral rectitude, which in this world, and that which is
to come, cannot fail greatly to affect their happiness and
well-being.[2]

Allen then advocates the standard deistic argument that
nature is the revelation of God. "As far as we understand
Nature," writes Allen, "we are [sic] become acquainted with
God."[3] Proof as to the existence of a Deity is adduced by observation of the order and harmony in the universe. "If we form
in our imagination a compendious idea of the harmony of the
universe, it is the same as calling God by the name of harmony,
for there could be no harmony without regulation and no regulation without a regulator which is expressive of the idea of God."[4]

Throughout *Reason, The Only Oracle of Man*, Allen inter-
sperses between the metaphysical arguments emotional and
poetic passages describing the beauty and perfection of nature.
For all their rather dry rationalism the deists were at times
capable of a rapture more commonly associated with pantheism
or mysticism. The following passage is an example of this
quality of deistic thought, and is a reminder that one should
not be completely taken in by the label of rationalism applied to
eighteenth-century deism.

By extending our ideas in a larger circle we shall perceive
our dependence on the earth and waters and the globe,
which we inhabit, and from which we are bountifully fed
and gorgeously arrayed, and nextly extend our ideas to the
sun, whose fiery mass darts its brilliant rays of light to our
terraqueous ball with amazing velocity and whose region
of inexhaustible fire supplies us with fervent heat, which
causes vegetation and guilds the various seasons of the year
with ten thousand powerful charms; this is not the achievement of man but the workmanship of God.[5]

In Allen's view the creation is moral; it reflects God's perfect
wisdom. The Creator, who is perfect, would not have created
an imperfect universe. Allen ascribes indirectly to the eighteenth-

century concept that this is the best of all possible worlds, when he says, in his involved and redundant language, that "God is unchangeable and infinitely just and good"; He cannot lapse from this perfect essence and his perfect attributes: "For all possible systems infinite wisdom must have eternally the best and infinite justice, goodness and truth approved it, and infinite power affected it."[6] The Calvinist conception of God is a perversion of His nature and an affront to human reason, writes Allen.

It is a selfish and inferior notion of a God void of justice, goodness and truth, and has a natural tendency to impede the cause of true religion and morality in the world, and diametrically repugnant to the truth of the divine character, and which, if admitted to be real, overturns all religion, wholly precluding the agency of mankind in either their salvation or damnation, resolving the whole into the sovereign disposal of a tyrannical and unjust being, which is offensive to reason and common sense, and subversive of moral rectitude in general.[7]

Allen also takes issue with the traditional Christian view that the Deity created the world out of a void, and thus existed before the creation. For Allen, the Creator and the creation are co-eternal and co-existent. He argues as follows:

God cannot in truth be said to be the first cause of all things. For, if by the succession of causes we could trace out the being of God, there would have been an eternity preceding his existence, . . . But although with propriety, God cannot be said to be the first cause, yet he is the efficient cause of all things, a cause uncaused and eternally self-existent.[8]

Therefore,

creation and providence or nature are as eternal as God. So that with respect to God and his works of nature there could be no first or last, for they are eternal.[9]

It is wrong, however, to assume that Allen and the deists *equate* God with nature as is the case with pantheism. Deism made clear distinctions between God and nature, and also, for that matter, between God and man, distinctions which later the transcendentalists tended to blur. In the following excerpt Allen is aware of the lure of the beauty of nature, and ends in a clear warning not to confuse "God with his works":

> The globe with its productions, the planets in their motions, and the starry heavens in their magnitudes, surprise our senses and confound our reason, in their munificent lessons of instruction concerning God, by means whereof we are apt to be more or less lost in our ideas of the object of divine adoration, though at the same time everyone is truly sensible that their being and preservation is from God. We are apt to confound our ideas of God with his works, and take the latter for the former.[10]

Allen, shifting his metaphor to Newton's, talks of the "machinery" of the universe, and the great "architect" who has so constructed it, that the machinery never be "altered or rectified."

> In vain we endeavor to search out the hidden meaning of perpetual motion, in order to copy nature, for after all our researches we must be contented with such mechanism as will run down and need rectification again; but the machine of the universe admits of no rectification, but contrives its never ceasing operations under the unerring guidance of the providence of God.[11]

Morality, for Allen and the eighteenth-century deists, was not based on divine revelation, but on the perfect and observable operation of the universe itself. "For as we learn from the works of nature an idea of the power and wisdom of God, so from our own rational nature we learn of his moral perfection." Man, then, unaided by any supernatural means, through his own rational nature, comes to understand the moral laws:

> we infer that all rational beings, who have an idea of justice, goodness and truth, have at the same time either a greater or less idea of the moral perfection of God.[12]

Morais, in his thorough and objective study of American deism, says that the movement was generally as cautious and non-revolutionary in temper as the eighteenth-century liberalism of which it was a part. "Although a few of its bolder spirits achieved some contemporary notoriety for their militant attack upon revealed Christianity, most of the deistic champions were willing to leave the question of divine revelation alone."[13] Morais includes many minor figures, such as "Hawley, a Northampton lawyer, Bliss, a New England clergyman, and Edmund Randolph, a prominent Virginia Statesman," who, he says, "eventually retraced their steps and returned to the Christian fold." The point to keep in mind, however, is that the three greatest exponents of American deism, Allen, Paine and Jefferson, were in varying degrees strongly opposed to revealed religion. Paine is most militant, Allen second, and even Jefferson, whom Morais calls a Christian deist, in much of his private correspondence is strongly antagonistic to many doctrines of Christianity. When the deists discussed the derivation of moral law they inevitably had to come to grips with historical Christianity, which held that the moral law was revealed to man by God through the medium of the Holy Scriptures. It was in this area that the more militant deists made their strongest attacks. The majority tended merely to point out the glory of the Creator as represented in His works, and were not brought into any significant conflict with traditional religion. Morais explains:

> Most American deists, therefore, contented themselves with the innocuous common sense truths of the pure and simple Religion of Nature, with its basic premise of a First Cause, its acceptance of a future state and its emphasis upon virtuous living.[14]

But Allen, Paine and, to a large extent Jefferson, were not mild and compromising men; they were forthright and outspoken thinkers. Allen expounds the standard deistic argument when he says that morality is derived from the perfection of the laws of nature through the medium of human reason:

> morality does not derive its nature from books, but from the fitness of things: and though it may be more or less interspersed through the pages of the Koran, its purity and rectitude would remain the same; for that is founded in

eternal right, and whatever writings, books or oral specula-
tions, best illustrate or teach this moral science, should
have the preference ... and as it [morality] is congenial
with reason, and truth, it cannot [like other revelations]
partake of imposture. This is natural religion, and could be
derived from none other than God.[15]

Morais points out that Allen's book was a significant swing
to the left, "a swing stimulated by the rising anti-clerical spirit
of the age." So vigorous was Allen's attack upon the priesthood
that he denied being a Christian "except as infant Baptism
made him so."[16]

Allen's argument against Christianity was based not only on
philosophical and theological differences, but on the latter's
claim of being the exclusive possessor of divine truth. Here
his vituperation knew no bounds, as the following example will
illustrate:

To suppose that God Almighty has confined his goodness
to this world to the exclusion of all others, is much to the
idle fancies of some individuals ..., that they, and those of
their communion of faith, are the favorites of heaven,
exclusively; but these are narrow and bigotted conceptions,
which are degrading to a rational nature, and utterly unworthy of God of whom we should form the most exalted
ideas.[17]

Allen felt that Christian revelation, and indeed, any religious
revelation, was blind superstition repugnant to the claims of
reason and common sense. Man by nature, he said, has an ability
to distinguish between right and wrong. This, says Allen, "is the
origin of moral obligation and accountability, which is called
natural religion." Furthermore, it undoubtedly was the "ultimate
design of our creator" in conveying upon us reasoning powers
and sensibilities, that we should serve and honor him with
these endowments: "and with those united capacities search
out and understand our duty to him, and to one another, with
the ability of practising the same, as may be necessary for us

in this life." Revelation is in error because "there is nothing beyond natural perception."[18]

> every kind and degree of apprehension, reflection and understanding, which we can attain to in any state of improvement whatever is no more supernatural, than the nature of man, from whence perception and understanding is produced, may be supposed to be so; nor has or could God Almighty ever have revealed himself to mankind in any other way or manner, but what is truly natural.[19]

Allen thus argues against revelation as "inspiration or immediate illumination of the mind." If one must use the term revelation, Allen would give it the following definition: "an assemblage or rational ideas intelligibly arranged and understood by those to whom it may be supposed to be revealed."[20]

What then follows is an attack upon the infallible authority of the Scriptures themselves. In addition to the argument mentioned above, Allen claims that "language and translation problems" are another serious barrier to the truth of the Scriptures. "There are insuperable difficulties in translating ancient languages; differences in language itself poses a problem."[21] Then there is human error:

> our being exposed to the villainous practices of imposters with a variety of other deceptions, blunders and inaccuracies, which unavoidably attend written and diverse or variously translated revelations.[22]

Furthermore, since "every individual of the human race is in special circumstances and individuality," it would seem requisite that each person should have his "particular and diverse revelation, in which his particular duty might be known in all cases."[23] One can see the absurdity of this argument.

What Allen is pointing at becomes increasingly apparent, and is reiterated time and again throughout *Reason, The Only Oracle of Man.* Since God is perfect and created a perfect cosmos, of which the individual with his reason alone can comprehend the moral and spiritual laws, it is not necessary to have a written document revealed to man to explain and promulgate these laws. This document is written by men and therefore subject to human errors already enumerated. The cosmos, or nature herself, is all we need to afford us a knowledge of God's moral and spiritual grandeur. Men do not need a Bible because they

> naturally understand moral good and evil, it renders such a book no ways essential to us, though it be admitted to be argumentative and instructive, it might like other sensible writings subverse mankind. But if it be defective in reason and interspersed with superstition, it would under the sanction of divine authority be vastly more prejudicial to mankind, than as though it were stamped merely by the authority of man; for an error in that which is received as infallible, can never be confuted or rectified; inasmuch as it usurps the authority of human reason.[24]

For Allen, natural religion precedes revealed religions. It is important to recognize this assertion in order to understand his term, "subsequent revelations." These, "whether denominational, external, supernatural, or what not, ... came too late into the world to be essential to the well-being of mankind, or to point out to them the only way to heaven and everlasting blessedness."[25] Another criticism leveled at these subsequent revelations is their provincial origins and national concerns:

> Besides, these subsequent revelations to the law of nature began the same as human traditions have ever done, in very small circumferences, in the respective parts of the world where they have been inculcated, and made their progress as time, chance and opportunity presented. Does this look like the contrivance of heaven and the only way to salvation? or is it not more like this world and the device of man.[26]

The "true, primitive, and supreme law," on the other hand, is no other than the "unerring reason" of the Deity himself. "This law is founded in nature; it is universal, immutable and eternal." It is not subject to any change from differences of "place, or time; it extends invariable to all ages and nations like the

sovereign dominion of that being who is the author of it." In
this way the Creator of all things "conducts the moral system
of being to the absolute perfection of his nature."[27]

Such a position regarding the origin and basis of moral law,
leads Allen to make his countless attacks upon the "absurdities"
of Scripture and the supernatural claims of religion in general.
Even granting the sublimity of the Decalogue, he argues, it
is a "mere transcript" of the original which has always been
in the possession of all nations. In another sense, his attacks
can be viewed as a manifestation of revolutionary democratic
thought, one aspect of which was to do away with priestcraft
and organized religion. Allen's arguments are thus similar to
those Paine was to expound some eight to ten years later:

> admitting those subsequent revelations which have more or
> less obtained credit in the world, as the inspired laws of
> God, to be consonent with the laws of nature, yet they could
> be considered as none other but mere transcripts therefrom,
> promulgated to certain favorite nations, when, at the same
> time all mankind was favored with the original. The moral
> precepts contained in Moses's decalogue to the people of
> Israel were previously known to every nation under heaven,
> and in all probability as much practiced by them as by
> the tribes of Israel. Their keeping the seventh day of the
> week as a Sabbath was an arbitrary imposition of Moses
> (as many other of his edicts were) and was not included
> in the law of nature.[28]

These positive injunctions cannot add anything to the law of
nature, because it contains in itself "an entire and perfect system
of morality." In addition, argues Allen, these commandments
cannot "enforce the authority" of the moral law, or confer any
additional moral obligation not inherent in the nature of things.
The obligation of natural religion "has ever been as binding
as reason can possibly conceive of, or the order and constitution
of the moral rectitude of things, as resulting from God can
make it to be."[29]

Later on Emerson was to formulate the idea that each revealed
religion was a partial expression of the Universal Law, or Over-

soul. In this aspect of his thought, Ethan Allen is Emerson's early forerunner, and, for that matter, as will be shown, most of the concepts advanced by the deists were to find expression later in the transcendentalists and Whitman as well. The following excerpt from *Reason, the Only Oracle of Man* could have been written by any of the deists or transcendantalists, and if it is not explicitly stated by Whitman, at least it is implied in his poetry. The point is a further development of the one just previously made, that no religion has an exclusive claim to divine truth.

> The natural law does not depend on the authority of Moses or any other legislator, short of him who is eternal and infinite, nor is it possible that the Jews, who adhere to the law of Moses, should be under greater obligation to the moral law than the Japanese; or the Christian than the Chinese; for the same God extends the same moral government over universal rational nature independent of Popes, Priests, or Levites.[30]

Regarding rites and ceremonies, Allen echoes Herbert of Cherbury and deistic thought in general; "they are not stable ... but change with customs, fashions and traditions and revolutions of the world; having no center of attraction, but interest, power and advantages of a temporary nature."[31]

To the Calvinist assertion that human reason is depraved and untrustworthy in matters of moral and religious commitments, Allen retorts that to admit to such a doctrine would ascribe imperfection to the Deity who created a perfect universe and perfect beings who inhabit it. However, unlike the later transcendentalists who deified man, Allen insists upon a difference between divine and human understanding.

> There is in God's infinite plenitude or creation and providence, such an infinite display or reason, that the most exhalted finite rational beings, fall infinitely short of the comprehension thereof.[32]

For the deists evil is not an absolute force in man or nature. Allen argues that to assume the existence of infinite evil alongside infinite goodness is a contradiction. God in his perfect wisdom could not have created anything but a perfect and good universe. Likewise, man himself cannot be depraved or sinful since he is a creature of God. But Allen does attribute the relative "evil" in the world not to God or the laws of nature, but to the "vicious agency of man," who sometimes perverts his godly reason and freedom to selfish ends. But this vicious agency is not the result of original sin (which is passive), but arises out of man's moral freedom to choose between good or evil.

> The freedom of our actions, from which virtue and vice become possible in the nature of man, was implanted in our minds coeval with the exercise of reason; or the knowledge of moral good and evil . . . our intuition of the reality of our liberty cannot be a deception, for it is the invariable voice of all rational nature that must have had the sanction of divinity intuitively promulgated to rational nature universally which lays the foundation of agency and consequently of accountability at the supreme bar of God . . . for it is disgustfully absurd to common sense to suppose that necessary benign beings should be rewarded for their destined or passive actions.[33]

Man, to use simpler, less theological language, is born guiltless; evil results in the wrong exercise of the God-given freedom of moral choice. Evil is therefore not attributable to the existence of a malignant force in the Universe. "Both the virtues and the vices of man are finite; they are not virtuous or vicious but in degree; therefore moral evil is finite and bounded."[34]

Another tenet of Calvinism that Allen attacked was predestination. He felt it was a preposterous doctrine not even worthy of dispute, for in his eyes it attributed moral evil to God's nature.

> To suppose the conduct or demeanor of mankind to have been predetermined by God, and affected merely by his providence, is a manifest infringement of his justice and goodness in the constitution of our mental powers in giving us a false and erroneous consciousness of guilt, thereby making us mentally miserable through deception, or mere

imaginary apprehension of vicious actions, in which we are wholly passive, ... therefore a predetermination of the actions of conduct of mankind is inadmissible, for it is injurious to the divine character to suppose it; as it would make God the author of moral evil to the exclusion of his offending creatures, or exclude moral evil from the universe; and if so, there need be no further dispute about it.[35]

Allen cites biblical references to document his attack on predestination. "Why did God hate Esau or punish Pharaoh?" he argues, "Were not their actions and deaths perfectly agreeable to his predestination, or will? And if so, why doth he yet find fault, for who has refuted his will?"[36] The Calvinists thus place themselves in an illogical and self-contradictory position when they say that man is predestined for damnation or salvation, and also maintain that man is a free agent. Allen analyzes the troublesome point as follows:

I believe that the God of Nature has so strongly implanted his law in the human soul, that the teachers of fatalism never erase it but conscience will forever give such teachers the lye ... though a part of mankind may, and have given assent to that unreasonable doctrine. Some advocates for the doctrine of fate also maintain that we are free agents, notwithstanding they tell us there had been a concatenation of causes and events, which has reached from God down to this time and which will be eternally continued that has and will control and bring about every action of our lives, though there is not anything in nature more certain than that we cannot act necessarily and freely, in the same action, and at the same time. Yet it is for such persons who have verily believed that they are elected (and this by a predetermination of God become his special favorites) to give up their notions of a predetermination of all events, upon which system their election and everlasting happiness is nonsensically founded; and on the other hand, it is also hard for them to go evidently against the law of nature (or dictates of conscience) which intuitively evince the certainty of human liberty, as to reject such evidence; and therefore hold to both parts of the contradiction, to wit, that they act necessarily, and freely upon which contradictory principle they endeavor to maintain the dictates of natural conscience, and also, their darling folly of being electedly and exclusively favorites of God.[37]

No tenet of historical Christianity was to go unassailed by Ethan Allen, least of all the supernatural and miraculous claims made by his inherited religion. The war over miracles had a long and continuous history in the religious development of New England. Indeed, the Puritans themselves were the forerunners of this theological conflict; Cotton Mather's later disavowal of spectral evidences in the Salem Witchcraft Trials, and Samuel Sewell's criticism of the judges may be said to mark the beginning of what in the transcendental period was to become a major theological pamphlet war between the Unitarians and their young wayward charges, Parker, Emerson, Ripley, and Brownson. The revolutionary democratic thought of the eighteenth century was extremely hostile to any beliefs which were removed from the dictates of reason and common sense. Therefore, their invective was particularly sharp when directed against the supernatural elements in Christianity. Obviously, miracles are absurd because they are an alteration of natural law, and to admit that natural laws can be violated, or disturbed, is to admit that these laws, ordained by the Deity are imperfect. Allen writes:

To suppose that God should subvert his laws (which is the same as changing them) would be to suppose him to be mutable.[38]

Allen is so certain of his position, and so assured of the absurdity of miracles, that in a somewhat whimsical mood he plays with the idea by constructing syllogisms, which he undoubtedly felt, as a rationalist, was uncontrovertible "proof" of his assertion.

God is perfect, the Laws of Nature were established by God; Therefore the Laws of Nature are Perfect.[39]

But, if we were to admit miracles, he says, the syllogism should be as follows:

The Laws of Nature were in their eternal establishment Perfect. The Laws of Nature have been altered. Therefore, the alteration of the Laws of Nature is imperfect.[40]

Allen felt that "magic, superstition all are connected with miracles," and that these have been "craftily imposed on the credulous," who are prone to believe anything, "marvelous, miraculous, or supernatural." He finds in those parts of the world where learning and science have prevailed, miracles have ceased to be believed, but in such areas of the world "as are barbarous and ignorant, miracles are still in vogue." Since in Allen's eyes religion and morality are rational and self-evident, miracles, even if believed in, can do nothing to improve man's moral actions.

> The premised, sudden, and miraculous alternation of the common course of nature might astonish us, but such alternations or changes, do not evince that they have anything to do with us, or we with them in the way of teaching or instruction; for truth and falsehood, right and wrong, justice and injustice, virtue and vice, or moral good and evil will remain so to be, and that independent of miracles or revealed religion.[41]

The deist attitude toward the founder of Christianity must now be taken into account. Throughout the history of natural religion as it developed in America, the common assertions held by its advocates in every period was that Jesus was a great ethical and moral teacher, but he had nothing of the supernatural about him. Jefferson took Christ to be the greatest of ethical teachers the world has seen, thus coloring his deism with more "primitive" Christian overtones. Paine and Allen, dwelt little upon the person of Christ, merely claiming that the teachings he promulgated were inherent in the nature of things and available to all who would exercise their own reason. For Allen, Christ could not be divine because

> it is impossible that God should suffer or change, or the person of Jesus Christ, as far as may be supposed to be of the essence of God; for the absolute perfection of the divine

nature exempts it from suffering, weakness or any manner of imperfection. Therefore Jesus Christ, in the nature in which he is premised to have suffered, could not be God.[42]

Similarly, the doctrine of imputation of sin is erroneous because "humanity obliges us to be kind and benevolent, but never obliges us to suffer for criminals," nor is it compatible with reason "to suppose that God was the contriver of such propitiation."[43]

On the subject of immortality, Allen has the following to say:

It is not contradictory to the order of nature, as far as we are acquainted with it, that our souls may survive our bodies and that they are by nature immortal and capable of existing in a mode and manner very different from this world.[44]

In his argument on immortality, Allen comes close to the Christian doctrine of future "rewards and punishments," for works and acts in this life. In a future state man must have "remembrance and consequently consciousness, that we are the same individual intelligent beings, who inhabited and actuated our respective bodies." This is necessary if we are to rectify ourselves from previous errors to gain felicity of mind.

We must then have a consciousness, not only of our identity of being, but also of our demeanor in this life; and thus by a retrospective consciousness, begin a condition of mental felicity of mental pungent woe, according to our works; which an awakened conscience, and the justice of God will disclose, at that important and dreadfull crisis of our unbodied and comprehensible existence ... should we admit that death extinguish the being of man, what narrow and contracted notions must we consequently entertain of God and of his creation.[45]

Closer scrutiny of Allen's remarks on immortality will disclose that he does not attribute the punishments, or rectification of the soul's transgressions in its earthly existence to any Supreme Judge; there is no concept of divine retribution. The new knowledge is obtained by the soul in reflecting backward upon itself and realizing its previous wrongdoings and then correcting them.

In his attack upon the Christian doctrine of rebirth Allen reveals more typically his distaste for institutional religion. There can be no mistake that he is referring to the Calvinist theology in this passage:

> In these parts of America, [the people] are most generally taught, that they are born into the world in a state of enmity to God and moral good, and are under his wrath and curse, that the way to Heaven and future blessedness is out of their power to pursue, and that it is encumbered with mysteries which none but the priests can unfold, that we must "be born again," and be regenerated; or, in fine, that human nature, which they call the "old man," must be destroyed, perverted, or changed by them, and by them new-modeled, before it can be admitted into the Heavenly Kingdom. Such a plan of superstition, as far as it obtains credit in the world, subjects mankind to sacerdotal empire; which is erected on the imbecility of human nature.[46]

Thus, Allen's *Reason, The Only Oracle of Man* based on the conviction of the sufficiency of natural religion was a repudiation of Christianity. To him, reason upon which true religion must be based, would lead mankind to worship and exalt God and to practice morality. Like his fellow deists, he accepted the existence of God and the human duty of divine worship. Virtuous living which conforms to right reason is conducive to happiness, and those practicing it will be rewarded here and hereafter. Since the religion of nature is rational, it is "universally prompted" to all men. In brief, Ethan Allen attempted to substitute for the particular revelation of Christianity, faith in the all-embracing reasonableness of natural religion.

CHAPTER TWO

Thomas Paine

"From 1789 to 1805, deism assailed more vigorously than ever before the supernatural revelations of Christianity."[1] Before the writing of Paine's *The Age of Reason,* deism was an aristocratic cult confined almost solely to the well-to-do classes. Paine's book marked a new departure in that the urban and rural masses were being reached for the first time. Unlike Ethan Allen's tract, Paine's writings were published in pamphlet form and were written in the kind of language that the average man could understand.

During and after the French Revolution the clergy united strongly in its opposition to the principles of political and religious freedom as expressed by the deists. Paine, long silent about the Church, felt, at last, that he had to make public now the ideals for which he had waited so long to be realized. Like Allen, Paine sought to discredit the clergy and undermine the Church by destroying the validity of Christian revelation. Paine argued that the Bible was not the word of God, but a very human document, one, in fact, disruptive of morality in many ways. Christianity was a sham perpetrated by the priests to control the minds and souls of the people. So profoundly shocked were the faithful by Paine's *The Age of Reason* that "its author was held with such deep and relentless hatred that his undeserved reputation of 'a filthy little atheist' has survived him by more than a century."[2] He was repeatedly described by his opponents as "an inveterate drunkard, a superficial reasoner, a malignant blasphemer and an impious atheist."[3] The vilification of Paine was due not only to his blatant and hard-hitting attack on Christianity, but to the fact that his writings were reaching the people. It was said that *The Age of Reason* could be found in every village in America, and that it was tending to "unchristianize" nominal believers. "Boys engaged in dressing flax, students enrolled in leading colleges, men enjoying the hospitality of convivial taverns were reading or eagerly discussing Paine's tract."[4] As a result, according to one account, tens of thousands defected from their faith. Morais says that the wide circulation of Paine's word was due to the fact "that it was brought to the attention of people through newspaper advertisements and orthodox replies; that it was distributed free of charge by deistic organizations; and that it was written in a style likely to be understood by the average man."[5]

Paine did not write *The Age of Reason* until he was along in years. He was too busy writing political pamphlets before and during the American Revolution. When Paine went to France to actively espouse republican principles, he was falsely accused by Robespierre of anti-revolutionary activities. While in prison he wrote his powerful and controversial book, which he felt would do for religion what the revolutionary ideas of *The Rights of Man* had done for the political emancipation of the common man.

It was not only the alliance of Church and monarchy (witnessed by Paine as a revolutionary republican in France) which caused him to break his lifelong silence on religious matters, but the growth of atheism. The latter, Paine believed, was endangering the existence of "the one only true religion"— deism. "To him disbelief in God and a future state was occasioned by the disgust men felt for the fanatical reactionary tendencies of the clergy."[6] Thus, Paine said he published the first part of *The Age of Reason* (1794) to save deism and republicanism.

Paine argued that the word of God was not to be found in any written or spoken expression, but in the creation itself.

Moreover, the account in the Bible was not binding upon future generations because it could not be regarded as a revelation, which, to Paine's mind, was a direct communication of God to man. The stories of miracles and prophecies were false because the former were contrived by imposters and were insulting to the Deity, and because the latter were vague and indefinite. These "evidences" having been added to "fabulous religion" were not necessary, but, in fact, derogatory to true faith. The genuine creed consisted of a belief in the existence of one God and the practice of virtue. Although not greatly concerned with the problem of a future state, Paine accepted the idea of immortality.

Thus, baldly stated, Paine's deism was not very different from Ethan Allen's. Both were the product of the Age of Enlightenment which believed only in reasonable and practical concepts easily understood by every man. Paine and Allen were both highly suspicious of any mystical elements in religious experience. The mythical or "fabulous" accounts in Christianity were hangovers from an early and superstitious period of history. However, their disregard of myth, which to the modern mind strikes a naïve note, should not stop us from overlooking the importance of these two books in the history of higher criticism of the Bible. The proponents of this criticism began to question the contradictory accounts in both the Old and New Testaments. Even their extreme view which considered Christianity nothing but a fabulous religion found expression in Ernest Renan and other nineteenth-century scholars who also considered Christianity to be a divine "mythus." Moreover, many arguments that appear in Allen and Paine are found in the latter transcendentalists, for they too opposed the miraculous and supernatural doctrines of Christianity.

In the preface to *The Age of Reason*, published nine years after Allen's book, Paine pays tribute to the French Revolution, which prompted him to write a "work of this kind."

> The circumstances that have now taken place in France of the total abolition of the whole natural order of priesthood and of everything appertaining to compulsive articles of Faith, has not only precipitated my intention, but rendered

a work of this kind exceedingly necessary, lest in the general wreck of superstition, of false systems of government, and false theology, we lose sight of morality, of humanity, and of the theology that is true.[7]

Paine asserts the principle of individualism in matters of religious belief. Historical faiths are in error because they seek to impose dogmas and theological doctrines upon the rest of mankind with unquestioning authority. The various churches perpetrate a holy lie to control and dominate the lives and minds of the people. Therefore, enjoins Paine:

I do not believe in the creed professed by the Jewish Church, by the Roman Church, by the Greek Church, by the Turkish Church, nor by any church that I know of. My own mind is my own church. All national institutions of Churches, whether Jewish, Christian or Turkish (Moham-medan) appear to me no other than human inventions set up to terrify and enslave mankind, and monopolize power and profit.[8]

When pure political freedom will prevail (Paine hoped as a result of the French Revolution) in the ensuing period of intel-lectual freedom, these doctrines, which he felt were false, would be detected and overthrown. "Man would return to the pure unmixed unadulterated belief in one God and no more."[9] It is necessary for his happiness that man be faithful to himself (Emerson's theme in "Self-Reliance"). For, said Paine, "infidelity does not consist in believing or in disbelieving; it consists in professing to believe what he does not believe."[10]

Another point regarding revealed religion which Paine attacks sharply is the claim by each of the religions that it is in special and exclusive possession of Divine Truth.

Every national church or religion has established itself by pretending some special mission from God, communicated to certain individuals. The Jews have their Moses; the Christians their Jesus Christ, their apostles and saints; and the Turks their Mohamet, as if the way to God was not open to every man alike.[11]

Paine goes on to say that each church has its own book of revelation. "Each of those churches accuses the other of unbelief; and for my own part, I disbelieve them all." This attack upon the spiritual exclusiveness of historical religions was a common idea held by the advocates of natural religion. They were opposed to this concept because it denied the universality of moral law which is inherent in nature and in man, placed there by the Deity Himself. Therefore, each man has within him the seeds of divinity, and the means of leading a moral life. Emerson was particularly insistent on this point; the individual confronting the Oversoul experiences within him the immanence of God. According to Paine, it is contrary to the "true religion" to take on faith the claims of prior revelations. That cannot be a true revelation, as the orthodox claim, which comes second hand to the believer. God can communicate His will to a person, says Paine, but the communication ends at that point; it is merely hearsay if that person tells of his revelation to others. Thus, Paine writes:

No one will deny or dispute the power of the Almighty to such a communication (revelation), if he pleases. But admitting for the sake of a case, that something has been revealed to a certain person, and not revealed to any other person, it is revealed to that person only when he tells it to a second person, a second to a third, a third to a fourth, and so on, it ceases to be a revelation to all those persons. It is a revelation to the first person only and hearsay to every other, and consequently they are not obliged to believe it. It is a contradiction in terms and ideas, to call anything a revelation that comes to us at second hand, either verbally or in writing. Revelation is necessarily limited to the first communication—after this, it is only an account of something which that person says was a revelation to him.[12]

With this line of reasoning Paine rejects the supernatural basis of Christianity, and for that matter, of any other revealed religion. He requires more proof than the account of the religious founder. "When I am told," says Paine, "that the Koran was written in heaven and brought to Mohamet by an angel, the account comes too near the kind of hearsay evidence and second hand authority as the former. I did not see the angel myself, and therefore I have a right not to believe it."[13]

Paine uses the same argument to cast doubt on the divine birth of Christ. "Neither Joseph or Mary," says Paine, "wrote any such matter themselves; it is only reported by others that *they said so*—it is hearsay upon hearsay, and I do not choose to rest my belief upon such evidence."[14] He accounts for the myth of the divine origin of Christ by saying that it was the current heathen mythology which dealt with the death and rebirth of the god which paved the way for the Christian belief. "Almost all the extraordinary men that lived under the heathen mythology were reputed to be sons of some of their gods. It was not a new thing at that time, to believe a man to have been celestially begotten. The intercourse of gods with women was then a matter of familiar opinion."[15] The Christian account of the miraculous birth of Christ was therefore derived from Greek and Roman mythologies, Christ replacing Adonis, and Mary, Diana. Paine's explanation of the deification of Christ and Mary anticipates the studies of some modern anthropologists and liberal theologians, notably Sir James Frazer in *The Golden Bough* and A. Powell Davies in his book, *The First Christian*.[16] The Christian godhead, according to Paine

> was no other than a reduction of the former plurality which was about 20 or 30 thousand; the statue of Mary succeeded the statue of Diana of Ephesus, the deification of heroes changed into the canonization of saints; the Mythologists had gods for everything; the Christian Mythologists had saints for everything; the Church became as crowded with one as the Parthenon had been with the other, and Rome was the place of both.[17]

The "Christian Mythologists" erected a fable upon simple narrative details "which for absurdity and extravagance are not exceeded by anything that is to be found in the mythology of the ancients." Paine's sarcasm and ridicule were used with devastating effect when he described the Christian account of the Fall and Redemption of man. It typifies not only Paine's strong feelings on the subject, but the eighteenth century's general distrust of myth and imagination. In this respect it deserves to be quoted at length.

> The Christian Mythologists, after having confined Satan to a pit, were obliged to let him out again to bring on the sequel to the fable. He is then introduced into the Garden of Eden, in the shape of a snake or a serpent, and in that shape he enters into familiar conversation with Eve, who is no way surprised to hear a snake talk; and the issue of this tete-a-tete, is that he persuades her to eat an apple which damns all mankind. . . . Having thus made an insurrection and a battle in Heaven in which none of the combatants could be either killed or wounded. . . . put Satan into the pit. . . . let him out again—giving him a triumph over the whole creation. . . . damned all mankind by the eating of an apple, these Christian Mythologists bring the two ends of their fable together. They represent the virtuous and amiable man, Jesus Christ, to be at once both God and man, and also the son of God, celestially begotten, on purpose to be sacrificed because, they say, that Eve in her longing had eaten an apple.[18]

And Paine concludes this discussion as follows:

> Putting aside everything that might excite laughter by its absurdity, or detestation by its profaneness, and conferring ourselves merely to an examination of the parts, it is impossible to conceive a story more derogatory to his powers, than this story is.[19]

Paine attacked the belief in Christ's divine nature because it is contradictory and absurd to reason. It makes of Christianity "a species of Atheism—a sort of religious denial of God." It professes to believe in a man rather than in God.

> It introduces between man and his maker an opaque body, which it calls a Redeemer, as the moon introduces her opaque self between the earth and the sun, and it produces by this means a religious or an irreligious eclipse of light. It has put the whole orbit of reason into shade.[20]

Paine, however, has nothing but great admiration and respect for the person of Jesus, despite his sharp attacks on the mysteries of Christianity. Paine speaks highly of the lofty character and ethics of its founder. Jesus is referred to as a "virtuous and amiable man"; the morality that he expounded and practiced was most ideal and "benevolent," and though similar systems of morality had been preached by Confucius and the Stoics, and in recent times by the Quakers and by good men in all periods of history, "it has not been exceeded by any."[21]

Because Paine does not consider the Scriptures in their historical context in his critique of the Bible, his impatience with the grosser elements in them reach great intensity. Again, it is well to remember that Paine is not primarily a scholar or critic, but a pamphleteer and propagandist. He is more concerned with moving people to action by shocking them through ridicule and exaggeration. No doubt Paine had strong feelings about the Bible, but it is essentially the hard-hitting advocate of republicanism and freedom who is speaking out against what he feels the clergy has used and is continuing to use as a means to control the minds and souls of men. Hence, in one place he refers to the Bible as an "obscene book," full of voluptuous debaucheries ... cruel and torturous executions." If we consider, says Paine

> the unrelenting vindictiveness with which more than half the Bible is filled, it would be more consistent that we called it the word of a demon than the word of God. It is a history of wickedness that has served to corrupt and brutalize mankind; and for my part, I sincerely detest everything that is cruel.[22]

Like Ethan Allen before him, Paine argues that the written word cannot be a vehicle for transmitting the word of God to man. "The continually progressive change to which the meaning of words is subject, the want of a universal language which renders translation necessary, the errors to which translations are again subject, the mistakes of copyists and printers, together with the possibility of willful alteration, are of themselves evidence that the human language, whether in speech or in print

cannot be the vehicle of the word of God. That what we call
the Old and New Testaments is in the same state as the original
version is very uncertain."[23]

To Paine the word "prophet" means nothing more than "poet."
Since the Hebrew word for prophet means one through whom
God speaks, the author of *The Age of Reason,* whose avowed
aim is to denounce the supernatural basis of Christianity, puts
prophets on no higher plane than artists or poets. Here again
there are striking resemblances between Paine's deism and
transcendentalism. Emerson said that the Bible was no more
the word of God than are the words of a great poet or philosopher. Indeed, the whole transcendental movement, according
to Perry Miller, represented the outpourings of a religious sentiment in literary form. The seeds of this idea already existed, as
shown, in the writings of the eighteenth-century deists. "A
prophet doesn't predict anything of the future," says Paine.
"Deborah and Borah are called prophets, not because they
predicted anything, but because they composed the poem or
song that bears their name in celebration of an act already
done."[24]

In his detailed dissection of the Old and New Testaments,
Paine finds them entirely lacking in authenticity. "He endeavored
to prove that Moses, Joshua, Samuel, David and Solomon did
not compose the books ascribed to them." In fact, the Pentateuch
was written "by some very ignorant and stupid pretenders to
authorship, several hundred years after the death of Moses."[25]
Furthermore, Moses could not be the author of the five books
ascribed to him. He could not have lived so long as to be able
to write of the events in the Garden of Eden and those in
Deuteronomy. Also the Bible text reads, "And God spoke to
Moses"; a person to whom a book is ascribed, writes Paine
(begging the point), would never refer to himself in the
third person.[26]

Paine argues similarly against the divine origin of the New
Testament. The gospels are "altogether anecdotal," for they
describe events "after they had taken place." And in the accounts

of the sayings of Jesus and the events of his life and death, there are many contradictions. Therefore,

> revelation is necessarily out of the question with respect to those books; not only because of the disagreement of the writers, but because revelation cannot be applied to the relating of facts by the person who saw them done, nor to the recording of any discourse or conversation by those who heard it.[27]

However, Paine's indictment of the Bible is not wholesale. He acknowledges that the "anonymous publication of the Psalms and the Book of Job have a great deal of elevated sentiment reverentially expressed. "But," he quickly adds, "they stand on no higher rank than many other compositions on similar subjects, as well before that time or since." The proverbs, likewise, he feels to be a highly instructive table of ethics, but they are "inferior in keenness to the proverbs of the Spaniards, and not more wise and economical than those of the American, Franklin."[28] Here Paine reveals an eclecticism which is characteristic of natural religion in general. His reflections concerning the relative merits of the Bible, compared with the scriptures and proverbs of other cultures, can also be found in Parker and Emerson.

The Book of Job, according to Paine, contains deistic elements. "Here is a book," he exclaimed, "that is free of superstitions and absurdities." Job's questions about the nature of God and divine justice approximates the "true religion." However, Paine is more optimistic than Job in his conclusions. To the question posed by The Voice out of The Whirlwind, "Canst thou by searching find out God?" Paine replies, unlike Job, in the affirmative. "Yes," answers Paine,

> because in the first place, I know I did not make myself and yet, I have existence, and by searching into the nature of things I find no other thing can make itself; and yet millions of other things exist; therefore it is that I know by positive conclusions resulting from this search that there is a power superior to all those things, and that power is God.[29]

These questions "were put to the reason of the person to whom they were supposed to be addressed"; therefore, Paine observes in the questioning spirit of the book the method of the "true religion."

Similarly, the 19th Psalm is another work in the Bible which, for Paine, represents deistic religion. The Psalm glorifies the creation as the handiwork of God, and God's goodness and perfection. It, like the Book of Job, contains no supernatural "absurdities." "Man can only reasonably discover God by the argument of the First Cause," says Paine. For it is only through the use of reason that man can discover God. Take away that reason and he would be incapable of understanding anything; "and in this case, it would be just as inconsistent to read the book called the Bible (with the exceptions alluded to above) to a horse as to a man."[30] The 19th Psalm and the Book of Job, then, are the only parts of the Bible "that convey to us any idea of God. Those parts are true deistical compositions, for they treat of the Deity through his works. They take the book of Creation as the word of God; they refer to no other book, and all the inferences they make are from that volume."[31] Paine states further:

> What more does man want to know than that the hand or power that made these things is divine, is omnipotent? Let him believe this with the force it is impossible to repel, if he permits his reason to act, his rule of moral life will follow of course. . . . The allusions in Job have all of them, the same tendency with this Psalm; that of deducing or proving a truth that would be otherwise unknown, from truths already known.[32]

From this point, which is a good three-quarters of the way through *The Age of Reason*, Paine begins to discuss in detail the "true religion." Historical Christianity having been sufficiently maligned, Paine takes up the banner for deism.

> How different is this (Christianity) to the pure and simple profession of Deism! The true Deist has but one Deity, and his religion consists in contemplating the power, wisdom

and benignity of the Deity in his works and endeavoring to imitate him in everything moral, scientific, and mechanical.[33]

For Paine, and the deists in general, the creation is the only true and real word of God that ever did or ever will exist. Everything else called the word of God "is fable and imposition."[34]

Science has opened to the religious imagination vast immensities of space: our solar system, distant stars, and planetary systems. It is preposterous, according to Paine, that traditional religion "forms itself upon the idea of only one world, and that of no greater extent of 25,000 miles. Alas! what is this to the mighty ocean of space and the almighty power of the Creator?" The immensity, omnipotence and benevolence of the Deity "becomes enlarged in proportion as we contemplate the extent and structure of the universe." The single concept of a solitary world circling in the vastness of space yields "to the cheerful idea of a society of worlds, so happily contrived as to administer, even by their motion, instruction to man."[35] We regard our own planet, teeming with abundance, but we forget to take into account how much of that abundance is due to the great quantity of scientific knowledge which the universe has unfolded.

Nature, then, is the only revelation of God to man because "human language is local and changeable, and is therefore incapable of being used as the means of unchangeable and universal information." It is only in the creation that all our conceptions of the word of God can be united. This is so, says Paine, "because the creation speaketh a universal language, multiplied and various as they may be." It is an unceasing entity that every man can comprehend. Contrary to the language of Scripture, "it cannot be forged; it cannot be counterfeited, it cannot be suppressed, it cannot be lost, it cannot be altered. . . . It preaches to all nations, to all worlds, and this *word of God* reveals to man all that is necessary for men to know God."[36]

Deism, in general, tended to be mechanical and rational, lacking in emotional power. But in the following excerpt, Paine, the epitome of common sense, reveals this poetic side of deism that is not too often noted. In *The Christian Philosopher*, Mather expresses this quality and Shaftesbury in the *Characteristics* engaged in this sentiment to an even greater degree. Paine writes:

> Do we not see a fair creation prepared to receive us the instant we are born—a world furnished to our hands, that cost us nothing? Is it we that light up the suns, that pour down the rain and fill the earth with abundance?[37]

What the author of *The Age of Reason* and advocate of natural religion in general argued for was that religion arises from the individual's own reflection and experience and not through faith based on authority. The deists claimed a person is religious when he contemplates the power and beauty of the creation and follows in his daily life the virtue that this reflection teaches him. For the transcendentalists, the individual becomes religious the moment he experiences a feeling of oneness with nature and the Oversoul. The deists followed the path of reason; the transcendentalists the path of intuition. But in both cases the religious state is achieved without the "crutch" of codes of morality or articles of faith artificially imposed. Natural religion, Paine said, would cause a "revolution in theology."[38]

> The very nature and design of religion, if I may so express it, prove ever to demonstration that it must be free from everything of mystery, and unencumbered with everything that is mysterious. Religion, considered as a duty, is incumbent upon every living soul alike, and therefore must be on a level with the understanding and comprehension of all. Man does not learn religion as he learns the secrets and mysteries of a trade. He learns the theory of religion by reflection. It arises out of the action of his own mind upon the things which he sees, or upon what he may happen to hear or to read, and the practice joins itself thereto.[39]

Another concept in which natural religion differs from orthodoxy is that man is not a sinful creature. For the natural religionist man is born good and the universe was created and is sustained by a benevolent Deity. The Christian theologians, however, explain that there is a "problem of evil" inherent in the nature of man: man is born with original sin. The story in Genesis of the Fall of Man is the ground on which this doctrine is based. The attempt to justify and explain the existence of evil has been a stumbling block in the formation of Christian theology. Indeed, it is only comprehensible in terms of the biblical myth. Frazer has compiled an enormous amount of evidence to show that this Judaic-Christian doctrine is not unique. Similar stories exist in the folklore of innumerable primitive societies. Paine is correct in arguing from the rationalistic point of view that the concept of original sin is "based on the flimsiest of grounds." It is one of the reasons for his condemnation of the church.

> The church estranges man from God—considers him and causes him to consider himself a miserable sinner who must repent and be redeemed by God—in truth there is no such thing as redemption, that is fabulous, and that man stands in the same relative condition with his Maker as he ever did stand since man existed, and that it is his greatest consolation to think so. . . .
> Let him believe this, and he will live more consistently and morally than by any other system; it is by his being taught to contemplate himself as an outlaw, as an outcast, as a beggar, . . . as one thrown, as it were, on a dunghill at an immense distance from his creator, and who must make his approaches by creeping and cringing to intermediate beings that he conceives either a contemptuous disregard for everything under the name of religion, or becomes indifferent, or turns what he calls devout. In the latter case, he consumes his life in grief, or the affection of it; his prayers are reproaches, his humility is ingratitude; he calls himself a worm, and the fertile earth, a dunghill; and all the blessings of life by the thankless name of vanities.[40]

And furthermore, Paine points out, "he despises the choicest gift of all, the *Gift of Reason*." Man endeavors to compel himself to believe in a system "against which reason revolts." Paine is striking out against the theological distinction between human reason which is finite and imperfect, and God's knowledge which is infinite and perfect. The theologians are wrong; they "ungratefully call it human reason, as if man could give reason to himself."[41]

Though he attacked the miracles in both the Old and New Testaments, Paine, nevertheless believed in a miracle—the miracle of life itself. Natural religion considered the earth, the heavens, planets, stars, the various forms of inorganic and organic nature, in a word the creation to be the greatest and only miracle. Whitman was especially vocal in this regard. No one of the figures included in this study glorified more the richness and beauty of the everyday world than he did. His poems are a paean to the creation.

Paine continues his attack on supernatural miracles by saying that "miracles are bad to use as evidence to prove anything." In the first place, when we use miracles for the sake of inculcating a belief, it "implies a lameness, or weakness in the doctrine that is preached, and in the second place it is degrading the Almighty into the character of a showman playing tricks to amuse and make the people stare and wonder."[42]

Paine derives his ideas on morality from the contemplation of God's benevolence and equality toward all creatures. Observing this we see that "we are called upon to practice the same towards each other, and consequently, that everything of persecution and revenge between man and man, and everything of cruelty to animals, is a violation of moral duty."[43] Morality artificially imposed through authority cannot then be true morality. However, Paine views the morality of the various institutional religions as relatively good or bad.

There may be systems of religion that so far from being morally bad, are in many respects morally good, but there can be one that is true; and that one necessarily must, as it ever will, be in all things with the ever-existing word of God that we behold in his works.[44]

What Paine is saying is one of the cornerstones of natural religion—namely, that all religions express part of an overall truth about man and God, and like his successors, the transcendental-ists,[45] envisions the unity of all religions in the future, stripped of their local and ritualistic differences, and stressing the insights which they all hold in common. Paine puts it as follows:

> It is certain that in one point all the nations of the earth, and all religions agree—all believe in a God; the things in which they disagree are the redundancies annexed to that belief; and therefore, if ever a universal religion should prevail, it will not be by believing anything new, but in getting rid of the redundancies, and believing as man believed at first. Adam, if ever there was such a man, was created a Deist; but in the meantime let every man follow, as he has a right to do, the religion and worship he prefers.[46]

In conclusion, Paine sought to destroy the supernatural basis of Christianity, only to propagate a universal religion based on the law of nature which each man could plainly understand. Moral duties, thus rationally derived, could be applied in daily life. He envisioned a synthesis of the historical religions which would bring together their moral and ethical concepts. Until that time each man was to follow the religion of his choice, with the ultimate *unity of all in view.*

Another important figure in eighteenth-century America who espoused very similar thoughts, though less publicly than Paine, was Thomas Jefferson, whose ideas on natural religion will be discussed in the next chapter.

CHAPTER THREE

Thomas Jefferson

Jefferson's position on natural religion "was typical of the American climate of deistic opinion, which desired the reformation and not the destruction of Christianity."[1] He was convinced that the real enemies of the teachings of Jesus were the clergy whom he proposed to strip of power. To accomplish this aim, Jefferson adopted a rather cautious approach—instead of aggressively assailing the biblical revelation upon which priestly authority rested, unlike Paine and Allen, he contented himself with drawing a distinction between "the religion of the priests and that of the Gospels." The first he desired to overthrow; the second, which he held to be natural religion, he wished to restore.

Jefferson was more of a scholar and more widely read than either Allen or Paine. He read Bolingbroke, Shaftesbury, Priestley, Voltaire and Rousseau among his contemporaries, and having a thorough classical education he was well steeped in the Greek and Roman moral philosophers and poets. He made ample use of these influences in the formation of his own philosophy.[2]

In spite of his familiarity with Voltaire, Jefferson's deism was not of the militant French school, but closer to the position of such English deists as Tindall and Chubb, who were anxious to save Christianity. Reason was to be the guiding light in the task of reforming the Christian religion, which was to be purged of its existing corruptions. Jefferson thought the moral system of Jesus "was the most benevolent and sublime probably that has ever been taught." The moral precepts of Christ, had been corrupted and altered by those "pretending to be his disciples." In reality these false prophets had

> disfigured and sophisticated his actions and precepts from views of personal interest, so as to induce the unthinking part of mankind to throw off the whole system in disgust, and to pass sentence as an imposter on the most innocent, the most benevolent, the most eloquent and sublime character that has ever been exhibited to man.[3]

Jefferson endeavored to recall Christians to the simple gospel first expounded by Christ. This gospel was in reality a restatement of the religion of nature, since it taught a belief in one God, the practice of virtue, and the existence of future state. For his deistic leanings, Jefferson was attacked by the New England clergy. Although described in 1784 by the Rev. Dr. Stiles as a "truly scientific and learned man—and very excellent," by 1800 he was characterized by the Congregational ministry as "the arch-apostle of the cause of irreligion and freethought."[4]

When still in his twenties, Jefferson collected under one heading gleanings from his classical and other readings. These were called his "Literary Bible" and were sententious excerpts mostly concerned with morality. The collection of notes starts off with passages from Herodotus regarding circumcision in Egypt (with a cross reference to Genesis) and Egyptian and Thracian ideas of immorality. Toward the middle it contains portions of Pope's *Essay on Man*. Reflections upon happiness, misery, friendship, death and uncertainty of an afterlife, the wisdom of renunciation, and the blessings of country life fill its pages. It is obvious that the young Jefferson was looking for a guide by which to measure his own moral and ethical development. In later life he was to make use of these ready and accessible quotations as an aid in the formulation of his own ideas. The following excerpt illustrates the trend his thinking was taking.

—Equality
which knitteth friends to friends
Cities to cities, allies to allies
Nature gave men the law of equal rights.
                    —Euripides, *Phoenissai* 5

His classical education and naturally critical and scholarly
mind went right to the fountainhead of knowledge and was
not content to rest on inferior sources and inaccurate translations. Karl Lehmann tells us that Jefferson aimed at assembling
various editions of ancient books which he studied comparatively.
He had taught himself to search for the exact meaning and to
use the tools of the professional philologist. He made a careful
study of the New Testament in Greek. In his advice to Peter
Carr he tells him to read the Bible "as you would read Tacitus,"
and to be critical of every doubtful event or episode, bringing
all before the bar of reason. He even tells Carr to question with
boldness the existence of God. The influence of natural religion
is, of course, unmistakable. He refers indirectly to Ethan Allen's
book, telling his correspondent that your "own reason is the
only oracle given you by heaven."[5]

Jefferson was charged by his critics of being anti-Christian
in his thinking. In a letter to Benjamin Rush in 1803, he answers
them indirectly by telling his correspondent that these people
know nothing of his opinions; that he is opposed indeed to
the "corruption of Christianity—but not to the genuine precepts
of Jesus himself."

> I am a Christian, in the only sense in which he wished
> anyone to be; sincerely attached to His doctrines, in prefer-
> ence to all others; ascribing to himself every *human*
> excellence; and believing he never claimed any other.[7]

In this same letter, Jefferson refers to a pamphlet by the
English Unitarian, Priestley, on "Socrates and Jesus Compared."
The pamphlet stimulated him to arrange in a "syllabus of outline,
the comparative merits of Christianity" with the ancient philosophers. At the beginning, he says he "eliminates all the

superstition and corruption of reason among the ancients endeavoring to present a fair, just view of their moral doctrines." In the ensuing comparison the ancients are called great in their precepts concerning control of the individual passions and excesses, that unrestrained would disturb our tranquility of mind, but they are deficient in developing our duties to others. "They embrace indeed, the circle of kindred and friends and inculcate patriotism, or the love of country in the aggregate, as a primary obligation towards our neighbors and countrymen they taught justice, but scarcely viewed them as within the circle of benevolence. Still less have they inculcated peace, charity, and love of our fellow man, or embraced with benevolence the whole family of mankind." As documentation, Jefferson in his characteristic mathematical listings, submits that out of ten headings in Seneca, seven relate to ourselves, two relate to others, and one relates to the government of the world. He makes a similar analysis of the writings of Cicero with comparable results. He calls somewhat incorrectly the system of the Jews deistic (probably meaning theistic)[8] and criticized them for their degrading and injurious views of God's attributes. Likewise, the ethics of Judaism are called "imperfect" and at times irreconcilable with the sound dictates of reason and morality." Jesus is called the great reformer, and his ethics the "sublimest eloquence." He corrected the "Deism" of the Jews, confirming them in their belief in one God and giving them more just notions of government and God's attributes. Jefferson is amazed by the fact that Jesus had such a profound effect upon the world since he, like Socrates, never wrote anything. He had not, like the latter, a Xenophon to write for him. Plato, the philosopher for whom Jefferson had the utmost dislike, "used only the name of Socrates to cover the whimsies of his own brain." He notes that all the entrenched men of wealth opposed Socrates "lest his labors should undermine their advantages." His teachings fell upon unlettered and ignorant men who wrote from memory, and long after the events. The teachings of both Socrates and Jesus have been disfigured by those sophists who came after them.[9] Those who tended to obscure by systematizing and perfecting the simple original precepts of these great moral teachers, and indeed all metaphysical philosophers, were the unending targets of his invective. It was part and parcel of the man's firm faith in human reason and common sense. Anything that was removed from the common man either intellectually or politically was evil and tyrannical.

Jefferson viewed Jesus as a sublime teacher whose moral doctrines, relating to kindred and friends, were more pure and perfect than those of the most correct of the philosophers, and greatly more so than those of the Jews; and they went far beyond both in inculcating universal philanthropy not only to kindred and friends, to neighbors and countrymen, but to all mankind. While the precepts of philosophy and of the Hebrew code laid hold of actions only, "he pushed his scrutinies into the heart of man; erected his tribunal in the region of his thoughts, and purified the waters at the fountainhead."

Jefferson drew upon these uncorrupted original doctrines of Christ in his famous "Bible where, after a critical study of the New Testament in Greek, he eliminated what he thought were the accretions of 'sophists and systematizers.'" He said:

I, too, have made a wee-little book from the same materials, which I call the Philosophy of Jesus: it is a paradigma of his doctrines, made by cutting the texts out of the book, in a certain order of time or subject. A more precious morsel of ethics I have never seen—[10]

Calvinism likewise suffers the strong condemnation of this free-thinking advocate of natural religion. The doctrines of election and human depravity were directly opposed to the idea that man is born good and has an innate moral sense as advocated by the believers in natural religion. Therefore, hostility toward Calvinism can be traced from the eighteenth and nineteenth centuries and, even into the twentieth century, in the poems of Wallace Stevens, despite the fact that Calvinism now holds none of the importance and influence that it held earlier in our history. In a letter to John Adams dated April 11,

1823, Jefferson calls Calvin an "atheist," and his religion "demonism." "If man ever worshiped a false God, he did—It would be more pardonable to believe in no God at all, than to blaspheme him by the atrocious attributes of Calvin."[11] In another letter to James Smith, the doctrine of the Trinity is referred to as "the hocus-pocus phantasm of a God like another Cerberus, with one body and three heads." He can't see how a rational person can believe such a paradox. "He who thinks he does, only deceives himself. He proves, also, that man, once surrendering his reason, has no remaining guard against absurdities the most monstrous, and like a ship without rudder, is the sport of every wind. With such persons, gullibility which they call faith, takes the helm from the hand of reason, and the mind becomes a wreck."[12]

Jefferson's ire was aroused when he spoke of theologians; and he was conscious that he was becoming more angry than his spiritual teacher would allow. Thus at the end of a letter to Ezra Stiles in which he had vented his spleen, calling the perverters of religion "crazy theologists which have made Babel of a religion the most sublime ever preached to man." He adds "I am sometimes more angry with them than is authorized by the blessed charities which he preaches."[13]

God, to Jefferson was incapable of being defined, and no attempt, he felt, should be made. "If we could all, after this example leave the subject as indefinable we should be all of one sect, doers of good and eschewers of evil." But he did speculate in his own way on the nature of the Deity. He held that when one takes a view of the universe in its parts, general or particular, "it is impossible for the human mind not to perceive and feel a conviction of design, consummate skill, and indefinite power in every atom of its composition; the movements of the heavens, the regulations of the tides, the distribution of the land and sea, the stars so exactly held in their course by the balance of centrifugal and centripetal forces." Everything down to the minutest detail, he says presupposes a Fabricator of the universe. "We see too, evident proof of the necessity of a superintending power to maintain the universe in its course and order."[14]

Jefferson, like the other deists, felt that man was born with a moral sense. Through the use of reason he should be able to lead a virtuous life. Thus he wrote to Dupont de Nemours in 1816 testifying to his belief that "morality, compassion, generosity are innate elements of the human constitution." If this is so, then, education and the appeal to reason should suffice without the introduction of supernatural terrors to reform the evildoers to the natural path of goodness. The sense of right and wrong "is as much a part of [man's] nature, as the sense of hearing, seeing, feeling; it is the true foundation of morality."[15]

Jefferson's thought is preeminently practical; he would have little to do with theories and concepts which were removed from the comprehension of the average man, or which were based on abstractions. In a letter to Peter Carr, 1787, he informs him that persons attending lectures upon moral philosophy largely waste their time. For the rules of our moral conduct are not a matter of science to be learned through the head, but are seated in the heart. For then only those men of science (knowledge) would be able to act morally.

He who made us would have been a pitiful bungler, if he had made the rules of our moral conduct a matter of science. For one man of science there are thousands who are not. What would have become of them? Man was to be destined for society. His morality, therefore, was to be formed to this object. He was endowed with a sense of right and wrong, merely relative to this.[16]

He then goes on to criticize thinkers who claim that the foundation of morality is in the Beautiful or the True (Plato). Jefferson's view was that truth is certainly a branch of morality, but that presented as its foundation it is "as if a tree taken up by the roots, had its stem reversed in the air and one of its branches planted in the ground." He is also critical of thinkers who posit self-interest or egoism as the basis of morality. We cannot owe any duties to ourselves in the strictest sense; obligation requires two parties. "Self-love, therefore, is no part of morality. Indeed, it is exactly its counterpart. It is the sole antagonist of virtue, leading us constantly by our propensities to self-gratification in violation of our moral duties to others." We do not, as Helvetius claims, gain pleasure from rescuing ourselves from the sight of an unfortunate spectacle by giving succor to the unfortunate object. These good acts give us pleasure, says Jefferson, but how does it happen that they give us pleasure? "Because nature hath implanted in our breasts a love of others, a sense of duty to them, a moral instinct, in short, which prompts us irresistibly to feel and to succor their distresses, and protests against the language of Helvetius."[17]

Like Shaftesbury, Jefferson claimed the moral sense may be exercised as may a limb of the body. While it is true that this sense is dependent in some degree to the guidance of reason, it is nevertheless a small stock which is required. "State a moral case to a ploughman and a professor. The former will decide it, and often better than the latter, because he had not been led astray by artificial rules." He then tells his young charge to read good books on this subject, praising the works of Sterne as a good guide to morality.[18]

One of the most important of his public proposals was the one on religious freedom, passed in the Assembly of Virginia in 1786. In his directions for his épitaph and tombstone, Jefferson listed this Bill along with the Declaration of Independence, and the Founding of the University of Virginia as the three achievements he wanted most to be remembered for. The bill is remarkable for its age and the liberal democratic attitude toward religion which it contained—"that all men shall be free to profess, and by argument to maintain, their opinions in matters of religion, and that the same shall in no wise diminish, enlarge, or affect their civil capacities."[19] For any act preventing him from declaring these principles or entering a public office because of his religious opinions is an infringement of his natural rights.

In summary then, we see Jefferson's early interest in the classical philosophers affording him a guide to his own moral development and a useful tool toward the formation of his mature moral philosophy. His preference for the ethics of Jesus attests to the profound concern he had that morality should not only be concerned with the government of the individual's desires and passions, but with our actions toward our fellow man. The pure moral system of Jesus is, to Jefferson, a sublime expression of religion based on reason and love of nature, and by adhering to it, the individual would be following natural religion.

CHAPTER FOUR

Philip Freneau

Though not a major poet, Freneau is included in this study because his poetry reflects, in varying degrees, the rationalism of his age. A contemporary of Paine and Jefferson, Freneau supported at one period of his career the current deistic spirit. However, he was a enigmatic figure whose ideas and attitude shifted throughout his lifetime. Nelson F. Adkins maintains that Freneau's thought reveals a mixture of "(1) orthodox religious belief based in part, on Biblical revelation; (2) the back-to-nature idealogy; (3) scientific deism; (4) Epicureanism and other classical doctrines." Adkins finds that it is difficult to classify him "as an active or militant deist like his contemporaries, Paine and Elihu Palmer." Most of his poems which contain deistic thought were not originally printed in newspapers or periodicals where they might have gained more attention, but appeared for the first time in the 1809 and 1815 editions of Freneau's works.[1]

Freneau's ideas on natural religion are set forth explicitly in his deistic poems entitled (1) "Reflections on the Constitution, or Frame of Nature," (2) "On the Universality and Other Attributes of God of Nature," (3) "On the Uniformity and Perfection of Nature," and (4) "On the Religion of Nature." They are reflected less explicitly in other poems as well. By 1800,

Freneau had entered upon a period of philosophical and religious reflection, and it is to this portion of his work the didactic poems cited above belong. They seem rather stereotyped, mainly patterned on the ideas set forth in Paine's *Age of Reason*. The religious principles expounded by the deists can be quickly summarized as follows: (1) Nature is the creation of a benevolent God; (2) the universe is a perfectly designed, harmonious whole, whose laws, conceived by God, work with unswerving precision; (3) a benevolent God created man who is therefore born good, and who should act with kindness toward his fellow man; and (4) man should endeavor to apply to the machinery of government the eternal and immutable laws by which the universe operates, and thus make possible a perfect society.

In the poem "On the Universality and Other Attributes of the God of Nature," Freneau expounds the deistic principle that the existence of God is proved by the observation of unity and harmony in the creation. Freneau writes:

> All that we see, about, abroad,
> What is it all, but nature's God?
> In meaner works discover'd here
> No less than in the starry sphere.
>
> In seas, on earth, this God is seen:
> All that exist, upon him lean;
> He lives in all, and never stray'd
> A moment from the works he made.[2]

The principle that man is born good and possesses an innate moral sense is expressed in the poem, "The Religion of Nature."

> Born with ourselves, her early sway
>   Inclines the tender mind to take
> The path of right, fair virtue's way
>   Its own felicity to make...[3]

Belief in the perfectibility of man is one of the important doctrines of the advocates of natural religion. The conflicts and "evils" that exist in society and in man's relation with his fellows are not an inherent part of the structure of the universe.

By following the true nature of things, the perfect and harmonious laws by which a benevolent and wise Deity created the world, and by which it continues to operate, man can eliminate all imperfections and usher in a new millennium. Freneau gives voice to these thoughts in "The Religion of Nature."

> Religion, such as nature taught,
>   With all divine perfection suits;
> Had all mankind this system sought
>   Sophists would cease their vain disputes,
>   And from this source would nations know
>   All that can make their heaven below.
>
> . . . .
>
> Joy to the day, when all agree
>   On such grand systems to proceed,
> From fraud, design, and error free,
>   And which to truth and goodness lead;
>   Then persecution will retreat
>   And man's religion be complete.[4]

Freneau's deism was probably an outgrowth of his interest in republicanism and revolutionary thought during the 1790's. In 1797 Freneau edited a publication called *Time-Piece*. The newspaper "was primarily concerned with instruction in what its editor was fond of denoting "genuine republicanism.""[5] Essays which appeared in it were entitled "On the Despotic Form of Government" and "On the Democratical and Mixed Forms of Government." "On Some Principles of American Republicanism" and Thomas Paine's "First Principles of Government" ran serially from May 8 to May 12. Rousseau's "Dissertation on Political Economy," and his essay "Of Political Religion" appeared in succeeding issues.[6] "No reader of the *Time-Piece* was to be left in any doubt of the rational basis on which its editor based his complaint against despotism in all its forms."[7]

When it was rumored that Tom Paine was to return to America from France, Freneau wrote in the *Time-Piece*: "It is intimated he has made many enemies in this country on the score of his *Age of Reason*. Let us therefore receive him cordially... in the name of common sense."[8] When Elihu Palmer, who preached natural religion, came to New York to organize the Deistical Society, Freneau signed a petition to allow him to speak publicly in the City Hall. The petition, however, was unsuccessful and Palmer was labeled "An Infidel" in the municipal files; the oration was given elsewhere and was published in its entirety in the *Time-Piece*. Freneau continued to support Palmer by carrying advertisements of Palmer's lectures on "Natural Religion Opposed to Supernatural."[9]

According to Lewis Leary, it can be supposed that Freneau became a member of the Deistical Society, which was attacked by its opponents as a "combination of treachery, of indulgence, of frenzy, intemperance and every species of polluted baseness, for the purpose of combatting religion, virtue and wisdom."[10] To Palmer, as to Freneau, as indeed to the deists in general, "reason would bring about freedom from degrading religious superstition in the same way that the American Revolution and the republican movement had accomplished political emancipation."[11]

Although Freneau wasn't a consistently militant deist, he did make several attacks on historical Christianity, calling the supernaturally based doctrines of that religion "dread superstitions—the worst plague of the human race."[12] In the poem "On Superstition," he spoke out against the abuse of reason. A religious system which reduces this faculty to a feeble light must be false and pernicious. Freneau writes:

> But man to endless error prone
> And fearing most; what's most unknown
> To phantoms bows that round him rise
> To angry gods and vengeful skies . . .
>
> The social tie by this is broke
> When we some tyrant god invoke;
> The bitter curse from man to man.
> From this infernal fiend began.[13]

Not only is belief in a vengeful, Calvinist God an abuse of reason, but to claim His arbitrary interference in the laws of nature is to attribute imperfection to the creation and its Creator.

Could he descend from that great plan
To work unusual things for man
To suit the insect of an hour
This would betray a want of power.[14]

In a poem called, "On A Book Called Unitarian Theology,"
Freneau stresses the Oneness of God. Two years later, he
satirizes the Christian conception of the Trinity as the worship
of three gods, "first, second, and third, whom they yet hold to
be one and the same."[15]

Freneau seldom declared himself directly on the subject of
revelation. Yet, many of his pronouncements regarding religion
imply a rejection of the doctrine of the divine inspiration of
the Scriptures. Occasionally Freneau parodied the Scriptures,
which strongly suggests that he did not hold the Bible to be
a divinely ordained book. In "The Jewish Lamentation at
Euphrates," Freneau rewrote Psalm 137 so that it applied to
the oppression of the Americans by the British, but he kept the
original devotional character of the Psalm. Another example of
Freneau's parodying of Scripture occurs in "Pythoria; or the
Prophetess of En-dor," which contains dialogue based on the
story of Saul, Samuel, and the witch of En-dor.[16] Freneau gives
the narrative a farcical ending:

> She knew her lord and king were nigh
> And so she made a dutchman's pye;
> Her tablecloth she did display
> Saul eats his fill ... and march'd away.[17]

In the poem, "Belief and Unbelief," Freneau once again
carries the banner of rationalism. Every belief should be tested
before the bar of reason. Conviction cannot take hold of the
individual "till evidence has done its part."

> On mere belief no merit rests
> As unbelief no guilt attests:
> Belief if not absurd and blind,
> Is but conviction of the mind.
>
> Nor can conviction bind the heart
> Till evidence has done its part

And, when that evidence is clear
Belief is just, and truth is near.

In evidence, belief is found,
Without it, none are fairly bound
To yield assent, or homage pay
To what confederate world might say,

. . . .

From this great point o'er looked or missed
Still, unbelievers will exist;
And just their plea; for how absurd
For evidence, to take your word.[18]

Freneau was at times capable of Paine's vituperation. In the following example, Freneau like the militant deists linked kings and priests in his attack upon tyranny.

Religion bought her potent aid
To kings their subjects degrade
Religion!—to profane your name
The hag of superstition came.[19]

And another dig at the clergy:

The churchman's horn has blown its blast
Things take a different mark.[20]

Freneau's anti-clerical utterances perhaps reached their height in the passage where he describes certain books of the Old Testament as "the annals of the Hebrew butchers in which may be found authentic accounts of, now and then eighteen to twenty thousand young children, having been cut to pieces of a morning by order of the Supreme Being."[21]

But Freneau was not as unwavering an optimist as some of his deist contemporaries. At various times he expressed his doubts regarding the beneficence of nature and the goodness of man. Man, as a part of nature, is entitled to peace and happiness only as nature herself maintains benevolence and operates continuously according to the perfect and immutable laws inherent in the creation. With man at the mercy of nature's occasional caprices and moods is there any chance of ultimate happiness? Is perfection possible? Freneau comes to the same conclusions as the other deists when they proclaimed "Whatever is, is right." Leibnitz is the originator of this idea, although Alexander Pope immortalized it. Thus, Freneau, in his poem, "On the Evils of Human Life," writes:

> The seeming ills on life that wait
> And mingle with our best estate
> Misfortune on misfortune grown
> And heaviest most, when most alone;
> Calamities, and heart oppressed,
> These all attend us for the best.[22]

In "On The Uniformity and Perfection of Nature" the same idea is set forth:

> In all that is, above, around,—
> All, nature made, in reason's sight
> Is order all, and *all is right*.[23]

The "evils" that we experience is harmony not understood. This concept was also enunciated by Emerson and the other transcendentalists. As Emerson put it, close up the universe exhibited imperfections; certain things seemed "sour," but when viewed from a distance nature was harmonious, and "at bottom moral." Whitman asserted the same idea, but not as explicitly. In his poem, "As I Look Out," he lists the evils he sees in American society: the corruption of politicians, the wrongs against Negroes, and the like. But he insisted that "there has never been any more perfection than there is now." Whitman felt that these evils will eventually disappear during the course of cosmic evolution, and the future fruition of spiritual democracy.

In one respect Freneau gives more ardent espousal to America's future than his contemporary fellow deists. With him begins the prophetic optimistic faith in the coming millennium he felt was soon to be ushered in, a belief which was later to infuse the transcendental vision and culminate in Whitman's impassioned affirmation. In the poem "The Rising Glory of America," written while Freneau was still in college in 1786, mention is made of a "new Jerusalem" which will be created in America.

> And when a train of rolling years are past...
> A new Jerusalem, sent down from heaven
> Shall grace our happy earth,—perhaps this land,
> Whose ample breast shall then receive, though late,
> Myriads of saints, with their immortal King,
> To live and reign on earth a thousand years,
> Thence called Millennium. Paradise anew,
> Shall flourish, by no second Adam lost.
> No dangerous tree with deadly fruit shall grow,
> No tempting serpent to allure the soul
> From native innocence,—A Canaan here.
> Another Canaan shall excel the old,
> And from a fairer Pisgah's top be seen
> No thistle here, nor thorn, nor briar shall spring,
> Earth's curse before: the lion and the lamb
> In mutual friendship link'd, shall brouse the shrub,
> And timorous deer with soften'd tygers stray
> O'er mead, or lofty hill, or grassy plain:
> Another Jordon's stream shall glide along,
> And Shiloh's brook in circling eddies flow;
> Groves shall adorn their verdant banks on which
> The happy people free from toils and death,
> Shall find secure repose. No fierce disease,
> No fevers, slow consumption, ghastly plague
> (Death's ancient ministers) again proclaim
> Perpetual war with man: fair fruits shall bloom,
> Nature's loud streams be hushed, and seas no more
> Rage hostile to mankind—and worst than all
> The fiercer passions of the human breast
> Shall kindle up to deeds of death no more,
> But subside in universal peace.[24]

In summary then, Freneau reflects little originality in his deistic thought. He seems to have echoed the ideas in Paine's *Age of Reason*. However, the portrait of the coming millennium in the "Rising Glory of America," is an early expression of an idea which was to be repeatedly reemphasized up to the Civil War, reaching its apotheosis in Whitman's poems.

Natural religion as expounded by the deists was changing in tone and texture in the early part of the nineteenth century. The growth of the transcendental movement infused greater dynamism into its essentially deistic ideas. Although the transcendentalists rejected reason—the prime instrument of the deists—they nevertheless retained and further developed the main concepts of deism. As illustration of this statement, we now turn to the writings of Theodore Parker, one of the most voluble exponents of transcendental ideas.

Theodore Parker

Parker's reading was formidable and far-reaching. He was an extremely energetic student of theology and German philosophy. In contrast to his fellow transcendentalists, Parker remained a minister in the Unitarian Church.[1] Consequently, his writings reveal a more specific theological terminology and orientation than Emerson's and others. However, despite his nominal position as a Christian minister, Parker's ideas are very similar to those of Emerson.

Parker advocated virtually all the tenets of the deists; he believed that the universe was created by a benevolent God whose handiwork is apparent in the perfect and harmonious operation of the laws of nature. He also rejected the supernatural basis of Christianity, asserting that "Christianity does not stand or fall on the authority of Jesus," but on his preachings. Theological doctrines have varied from generation to generation, he asserted, but the eternal simple truths that its founder taught are the "Permanent" elements in Christianity. Parker was highly critical of those doctrines of the Church which were supernaturally derived. These "Transient" elements worked to the detriment of mankind causing conflicts and creating barriers to an understanding of true religion. His arguments, in this regard, duplicate those of Paine, Jefferson, and the other deists.

He, too, states that the "creation is the Scripture of God," that man is innately good, and that the universe, basically, is moral. Like Paine, Parker looks forward to the coming of the true natural religion which will dissolve all sectarian and theological perversions of historical Christianity.

Parker, however, differs somewhat from the other transcendentalists in that he does not stress instinct or intuition. He is less mystical, therefore, than Emerson or Alcott who felt that man reached God in those moments of deepest meditation where unity of vision is attained. Parker, then, can be viewed as a transitional figure between deism and transcendentalism.

The prevailing creed of New England at the time of Parker and the transcendentalists was Unitarianism. The transcendentalists for the most part were young ministers, graduates of the solidly Unitarian Harvard Divinity School. They became impatient with the mild, rational faith of the Unitarians and sought a deeper more satisfying religious experience. Perry Miller states that although the transcendental movement was literary in scope and form, it was essentially a religious revolution against the prevailing Unitarian creed. A study of transcendentalism shows that it was a further development of deism in terms of the specific moral and theological problems of the 1830's and 1840's. The young Unitarian ministers rebelled against what they termed the sterile and shallow faith of their elders. The Unitarians had adapted the rationalistic arguments of Locke to Christian dogma. Andrews Norton's book, *The Genuineness of the Gospels* (1837), which sought to prove that the Scriptures were divinely ordained and which was considered to be the culmination of Unitarian scholarship, was maligned in periodicals by the fast-growing group of young transcendentalists. They argued that Locke was wrong, that Christianity could not be summarized by rational arguments and demonstration. Soul could not be derived from sense, as John Locke and Andrews Norton had proclaimed. The truths of religion lay deeper and were only to be attained by intuition. The intellect, they felt, could operate successfully upon the everyday world of sense; in matters of religion it was of little use. Their terms were, in the light of rationalism, misleading. They defined the logical deductive faculty as "Understanding" (after Kant and Coleridge). "Reason," on the other hand, was overall vision, or intuition, man's spiritual awareness of God's moral law. Emerson and Jones Very were probably the most antirational of the transcendentalists.

Despite their aversion to rationalism, the transcendentalists would only oppose the rationalism of Unitarianism, not the rationalism of deism. In fact, they consciously or unconsciously made all the points that the deists had made earlier in their attack on historical Christianity. What they brought to natural religion was more fervor and a deeper emotional or mystical quality. Natural religion under the transcendentalists became infused with Neoplatonic and oriental ideas. The God of the deists was, in the main, aloof from his creation. Parker insisted that the deists had created one God who ruled over nature and another who ruled over human affairs. He felt that between these two conceptions or functions of God there was a "collision and a quarrel." The world governor "must interfere with the work of the world maker."[2] The transcendentalists wanted to reassert the ancient Neoplatonic and oriental, specifically Brahministic, idea that God is pure spirit who not only transcends the universe, but who is immanent and pervades every particle of both organic and inorganic nature. Furthermore, transcendentalism viewed God not so much as a static being or conception, but as a dynamic one. The universe was constantly coming closer to the central perfection of the Oversoul. Emerson considered nature to be a somewhat lesser perfection than God, and being so, the creation was always trying to reach the central perfection of its source. Parker, however, did not go so far as Emerson in the latter's Neoplatonic, Brahministic conception of the Oversoul; he clung to an essentially rationalistic, deistic view of God.

Parker sets forth his ideas on natural religion in his essays, "Theism, Atheism, and the Popular Theology" and "The Transient and the Permanent in Christianity." The first expounds the true natural religion (theism), and shows its superiority to both atheism and historical Christianity (popular theology). The second essay distinguishes between the moral and ethical precepts of Christ, which Parker calls "permanent" Christianity, as opposed to the variations in dogma and theology, which he terms the "transient" element in Christianity. "Looking at the word of Jesus, at real Christianity, the pure religion he taught, nothing appears more fixed and certain. . . . But looking at the history of what men call Christianity, nothing seems more uncertain and perishable."[3] Likewise, atheism is a dismal conclusion to man's religious thinking, for although he has freedom where the "popular theologian has not; freedom from fear, freedom to use his faculties—the theory of the atheist abuts in selfishness, and in darkness his little light goes out."[4]

But the true "theism" (natural religion) says Parker, is one in which the pure untrammeled ethical doctrines of Jesus are seen to teach the same as the religion of nature expounded by deist and transcendentalist alike. The whole world is to be a "Scripture" of God; "nature the prose, and man the poetry of God."

> The world is a volume holier than the Bible, old as the Bible, old as creation. What history, what psalms, what prophecy therein! What canticles of love to beast and man! not the "Wisdom of Solomon" as in this apocraphi [*sic*], but the Wisdom of God, written out in the great canon of the universe.[5]

The material world, then, is good and beautiful. There is no haphazard concourse of atoms which the atheist talks of; "there is no universe of selfishness, no grim despot who grinds the world under his heels, and then spurns it off to hell, as the popular theology scares us withal." God is present in the largest and smallest forms of nature, and the scientist studies God with his telescope and microscope.

> Everything is a thought of Infinite God. And in studying the movements of the solar system, or the composition of an ultimate cell arrested in a crystal, developed in a plant; in tracing the grains of phosphorous is the brain of man; or in studying the atoms which the fusiloil in a drop of

ether, or in the powers, and action thereof—I am studying
the thought of the Infinite God.[6]

Parker refers again to the old deistic argument of the universe
as the revelation of God when he contrasts the popular theology
(actually Calvinism in this passage) with "natural human
religion."

From behind this dark and thundering cloud of the popular
theology, how beautiful comes forth the calm, clear light
of natural human religion, revealing to us God as the
Infinite Father, as the Infinite Mother of all, perfectly
powerful, perfectly wise, perfectly just and loving, and
perfectly holy too! Then how beautiful is the universe! It
is the great Bible of God, material nature is the Old
Testament, millions of years old, spangled with truths under
our feet, sparkling with glories over our heads: and human
nature is the New Testament from the Infinite God, everyday revealing a new page as Time turns over the leaf.[7]

The God that Parker here envisions does not act by miracles,
but by universal law. Traditional religion is erroneous in teaching that God makes His will known to man through alteration
of natural law. The stories of His being present in a burning
bush, of issuing, through the fire and thunder on Mount Sinai,
a code of morality to Moses, bringing back Lazarus from the
dead, or the resurrecting of Christ—all are vestiges of an earlier
age of superstition and magic. This belief in miracles is destined
to perish in the light of scientific knowledge. These "transient"
elements and accretions steer men away from the true knowledge
of God and a virtuous life. They make of Him a wonder-worker
and magician, not the God of benevolence and perfection who
is the creator and sustainer of the universe. They are contradictions of God's perfect nature. Thus Parker writes:

Now God, in as much as He is God, acts providentially in
nature, not by miraculous fits and starts, but by regular
and universal laws, by constant modes of operation, and
so takes care of material things without violating their constitution, acting always according to the nature of the things
which He has made.[8]

Furthermore, traditional religion is wrong in assuming that God was present only with the Hebrews and early Christians, and is not now present in human affairs. The natural religionist asserts that God is ever present in human affairs, and concerns himself equally with the history of all peoples. To the claim of "special providence" made by historical Christianity, Parker replies:

> Theologians love to think that God was present with the Hebrews in their march out of Egypt at Mt. Sinai; that their exodus and legislation were providential. It is all true; but the same providence watched equally over the English Puritans, over the British Parliament making laws at Westminster, the American Congress at Philadelphia and Washington. It is well to see this fact in Hebrew history; well, also to go forward and see it in all human history, and to know that human nature is divine providence.[9]

Parker felt that the "modern notion of a special providence, wherever God acts without law, or against law, is the most spiritual and attenuated form of the doctrine of miracles." He predicted its end, and with it the end of the traditional faith ("the last glimmering of the candle before it goes out"), for it is an erroneous doctrine which denies the truth and wisdom of God to other races and creeds. This theological argument runs as follows: "The forms of religion in China, India, Egypt, Greece and Mexico, came by the *general* providence of God, growing out of the nature of man or coming at the instigation of the devil; while the Hebrew and the Christian forms of religion came by His *special providence* started in God, and were miraculously transplanted in human soil."[10] Certain Christians are still thought, says Parker, "more eminently under God's special providence." They are the "elect" and the world apparently was made for them. How can we reconcile this attitude with that, for example, of the "Mohametan who thinks the same of his form of religion and of the elect Mussulmans." This same criticism of the Judaic-Christian claim to exclusive possession of God's favor and grace had been made by Ethan Allen and Paine.[11] It is one of the points that led Herbert of Cherbury to draw up a list of common notions that would show the similarities, not differences in the historical faiths, and thus attempt to draw them together. At the base of all natural religion is the vision of a universal belief that would bind all nations and creeds in one human family.

Parker's attacks on the Calvinistic conception of God were made unceasingly and unsparingly. "God is not a great potter who molds human beings like clay, to do with them as he pleases." He does not cast the greater portion of them into endless misery and torment, as "it is taught in the greater part of Christendom." The theology that says that "God has a natural right to destroy the majority of mankind in this way, and that man has no right but to the caprice of God," Parker finds "odious." He cannot see how man can believe in such an idea of God and still call him good. This grim conception works havoc with "men's moral convictions." The Church, by teaching "infinite might is infinite right" depicts a God "who repudiates his own justice."[12] In the next passage he attacks the doctrine of election. He quotes Edwards to show the perverseness of such a theological conception. "Edwards," said Parker, "says that the elect are very satisfied with hell as the portion for their neighbors." Continuing to quote Edwards, he adds:

> The destruction of the unfruitful (and the unfruitful are those not elected to eternal bliss) is of use to give the saints a greater sense of their own happiness and of God's grace to them. The damned shall be tormented in the presence of the holy angels, and in the presence of the Lamb.[13]

In expounding his conception of a benevolent Deity, Parker often talks in terms of the rights and privileges accorded to man by the Declaration of Independence. Thus, Parker states that man has "a natural and inalienable right to the providence of the Infinite God."[14] God, then, was not an all-powerful, arbitrary ruler but a kind and tolerant Father who entered into contracts on a virtually equal footing with man. Here is Parker's view of the relationship of God with man.

The infinite God is infinitely bound to provide for his creatures, inasmuch as He is Infinite God, infinite Providence is the Divine function—A duty involves reciprocal obligation; a right is the correlation of a duty. There is a human duty to obey, reverence, and love God, with our finite nature, but also and just as much is there a human right to the protection of God. So there is a divine duty on God's part of providence toward man, as well as a divine right of obedience from man. I mean to say, as it belongs to the finite constitution of man to obey, reverence, and love God—the duty of the finite towards the Infinite; so it belongs to infinite constitution of God to provide of man— the duty of the infinite towards the finite. Obedience belongs to man's nature, providence to God's nature. We have an inalienable lien upon His infinite perfection.[15]

It is difficult, in reading some of Parker's pronouncements, to see how he could have remained within the fold of the Unitarian Church. While it is true that the Unitarians renounced the grim doctrines of election and human depravity, they still claimed that man was a finite and imperfect creature and needed the grace of God to ensure his salvation. They also held Christ to be a divine mediator between God and man. Both doctrines seem to be at odds with Parker's convictions. In "The Transient and The Permanent in Christianity" he attacked the supernatural basis of historical Christianity. Parker said it is based on "two pillars" which are doomed to fall: (1) a "finite" view of God, and (2) a "supernatural Christ." Traditional religion is

grim, it is awful. It bears great truths in its bosom, and those truths will last forever, but the popular theology as a system must fall. It rests on two columns. One is the idea of an angry God, imperfect in wisdom, in power, in justice, love, holiness; a finite, jealous and revengeful God; creating man from mean motives, for a mean purpose, and from mean material—God with a hell under his feet, paved with the skulls of infants not a span long, and full of horrid writhing life, that chokes it to the brim.

On the other pillar is the idea of a supernatural Christ, a God, and yet a man, with a supernatural birth, supernatural works, resurrection and ascension, a supernatural atoning sacrifice to take away the sins of the world. These are the Jachim and Boaz of this theology.[16]

Parker declared that the truth of Christianity did not rest on the authority of Jesus, but on the truth of his sayings. He viewed Jesus as a great ethical teacher whose morality was most sublime. In this respect, he resembles Jefferson among the deists. Jesus taught the "love of God, the love of man." The form it demanded is "a divine life; doing the best thing in the best way for the highest motives; perfect obedience to the great law of God." Its sanction is the voice of God in your heart, the perpetual presence of Him who made us and the stars over our head. But, at other times Parker could temper this unqualified view of Jesus, as he does in the following excerpt, which stresses the human aspects of Christ:

Jesus looked to God for his truth, his great doctrines, not his own private, personal ones, depending on his idiosyncracies and therefore only subjectively true, but God's universal, everlasting, the absolute religion. I do not know that he did not teach some errors also along with it. I care not if he did. It is by his truths that I know him.

No wonder then, that men soon learned to honor Jesus as a God, and then as God himself. Apostolical and other legends, let men believe of these things as they will. To me they are not truth and fact, but mythic symbols and poetry.... That God has yet greater men in store, I doubt not; to say this is not to detract from the majestic character of Christ, but to affirm the omnipotence of God. When they come, the old contest will be renewed; the living prophet stoned—the dead one worshipped.[17]

But Parker makes a very interesting point in his argument against supernatural beliefs when he says, "Is there any reason why moral and religious truths should rest for their support on the personal authority of their revealer, anymore than the truths of science on he [sic] who makes them known first or more clearly?"[18] in this manner he equates religion and science, insofar as they both are a function of *human* effort to wrest knowledge from the unknown. Religion, therefore, is not any more divine than science; rather the nature of its truth is concerned with a different area of human experience. Thus he can say:

> We never are Christians as he was Christ, until we worship as Jesus did, with no mediator, with nothing between us and the Father of All.[19]

Traditional Christianity has always stood in the way of scientific progress because it based "truth" on authority, not knowledge. Parker cites specific examples of the Church's conflict with scientists. "Galileo must have had to subscribe to the Ptolmaic system of the universe or be burned at the stake. The Jesuits who edited Newton's 'Principia,' said that his theory was contrary to theology and they published his mathematical demonstration of the revolutions of the earth only as a hypothesis, a theory, not a fact." In regard to the scientific estimates of the age of the earth, the Church finds itself in error when it claims the earth to be approximately 6000 years old, the figure arrived at from the time of creation in Genesis. The scriptural story of the creation of man and woman is also preposterous along with the claim that God favored one people over the rest of humanity. Parker, in the footsteps of Paine, asserts the following:

> About 6000 years ago God created one man, and out of one of his ribs formed one woman—the human race descended from that person.... God chose one family out of all the rest, made a bargain with them, revealed Himself to them, and not to the others, and loved them while he hated the rest.[20]

Another point on which Parker set his critical gunsight is "conscience." He held that popular theology tends to remove from man the God-given ability to judge between right and wrong. The Bible, Parker reiterates, "is full of blessed things," but it should not be held up as the ultimate recourse; it is no master. "It contains the opinions of forty or fifty different men,

the greater part of them living four to ten hundred years before
Jesus, and belonging to a people we should call half-civilized."
For example, in matters of capital punishment where open
disagreement exists as to the justice of taking one man's life
for another's, Parker shows that men adhere to capital punishment not out of their own soul-searching judgment, but simply
because the Bible says they should.

> If you should ask, is it right for the community to kill a man
> who has slain one of his neighbors, when the community
> have caught and put him in jail, and can keep him there
> all his life, shut from doing harm? The theologian sends you
> to the Bible, and tells you that once, (nobody knows when)
> somebody (nobody knows who), in some place, (nobody
> knows where) said, "Whoso sheddeth a man's blood, by
> man shall his blood be shed!"—and therefore to the end of
> time, you shall hang every murderer.[21]

Parker, an ardent abolitionist, strikes out hard against the
justification of slavery in the Bible to which some theologians
refer. "You ask," he says, "is it right to catch a dark-colored
man and make him your slave for life?" Theology answers, "Yes,
for Abraham did so even with white men, and everything that
Abraham did, of course, was right."[22] The issue of slavery gives
rise to Parker's use of ridicule and sarcasm used so effectively
by the militant deists. In the following passage he attacks the
hypocrisy of practicing Christians and the justification of slavery
by use of biblical "evidence."

> Religion is a most excellent thing in all matters except slave
> trading; there it makes men mad. Let us not apply religion
> to the "patriarchal institution," the clergyman answers. . . .
> Christ Jesus says nothing against the worst evils of Grecian
> or Roman slavery—not a word against buying slaves, breed-
> ing slaves, selling slaves, beating slaves, or putting them
> to death. It is plain that he approved of the institution, and
> designed that it should be perpetual. The great apostle to
> the Gentiles sent back a runaway slave, thus executing the
> fugitive slave act of those times, and giving an example to
> Christians "to fulfill all righteousness." It is only *natural*

religion which forbids slavery, the heathenism of pagan Seneca and Modestinus. Christians are not in a state of nature, but of grace. One of the advantages of a revelation is this—the kidnapper may keep his bondmen for ever. Mr. Jefferson said all men are created equal, and endowed by their creator with certain natural and inalienable rights, amongst them are the rights of life, liberty, and the pursuit of happiness. He was an infidel stumbling by the light of nature; but we have a more excellent way, and hold slaves by divine revelation which transcends the light of nature.[23]

In a passage in "The Transient and The Permanent in Christianity," Parker discusses the influence of the higher criticism on his own thinking about the authenticity of the Bible. It confirmed his viewpoint that it was no longer possible to believe in the miracles or the supernatural basis of the Scriptures. "One writer, not a skeptic, but a Christian of unquestioned piety, sweeps off the beginning of Matthew." Another scholar finds the latter portion of St. John of dubious authenticity. Many more such "errors of doctrine and errors of fact" may be found throughout the New Testament. We see how opinions have changed since the Apostles' time, "and who shall assure us that they were not sometime mistaken in historical as well as doctrinal matters . . . and that the fancy of these pious writers never stood in place of their recollection?" However, he argues, "What if this should take place?" Is Christianity, then, to be totally disproved? It must be so if it completely rests on a foundation which a scoffer may shake or which careful critics invalidate. But this is the foundation not of Christianity, but of theology. Christianity "does not stand or fall with the infallible inspiration of a few Jewish fishermen. Christianity does not stand on the infallible authority of the New Testament. It merely depends on these records for the historical statements of its facts. In this we do not require infallible inspiration on the part of the writer, more than in the record of historical facts." It is presumptuous for the believer to claim these recollections of the Apostles for the truth of Christianity, as it is equally absurd for the skeptic to demand that the New Testament support historical fact. The doctrines respecting Scripture have changed often; yet men lay great store in them. Some cling to these notions as if they were Christianity itself. It is over these points that theological battles are fought from age to age. "Some men have regarded it [the Bible] as the heathen their idol or the savage his fetish. They have subordinated reason, conscience, and religion to this."[24]

Parker, as he studied and reflected, began to think of religion in evolutionary terms. In discussing the history of religion, he saw a pattern of development. The savages had their fetishes, idols, and taboos. Pantheism similarly saw "blades of grass" as symbols of God's presence; and even though Christianity was a great advance, Catholicism still makes use of statues of saints and medallions in worshiping God. Thus, according to Parker, religion developed according to the following order: fetishism and polytheism, pantheism, and monotheism.

> The notion that God continually watches over the creation and all of its contents is one very dear to mankind. It appears in all forms of conscious religion. The worshipper of a fetich [sic] regards his bit of wood or amulet as a special providence working magically and exceptionally for his good alone. Polytheism is only the splitting up of the idea of God into a multitude of special providences, each one a sliver of deity.... Thus man has parcelled out the glorious name! The Catholic invokes his patron saint, who is only a rude symbol and mint-mark of that Providence which is always at hand. Pantheism puts a Providence in every blade of grass, in each atom of matter.... In virtue of the functions of providence ascribed to God, He is called by various names.[25]

Parker continues to trace the history of the idea of God in the mind of man in the Old and New Testaments. Thus, he finds in the Old Testament the idea of God as a "King," with men as his subjects. In the New Testament God is depicted in many instances as a "Father who rules His children for their good; restrains that He may develop, and seemingly hinders that He may really help." Parker points out, however, that the New

Testament is not more unique in this respect than the Old, and "the cruel God appears often in the Gospels, the Epistles and the Apocalypse not as a Father, but only a Lord and a King, exploiting a portion of the human race with mercilous rapacity."[26]

In another passage in his voluminous writings dealing with the evolutionary aspect of religion, Parker sees his own times as part of a continuous spiritual movement. Religion goes on "leafing and flowering" into new forms.

> The last three generations have done more than any six before in science, letters, art, religion, and the greatest art of bearing men and building them into families, communities, nations, and the human world. The religious faculty vegetates into new churches, animates into new civilization, men and women. Tell me of Moses, Isaiah, Confucius, Zoroaster, Buddha, Pythagoras, Jesus, Paul, Mohamet, Aquinas, Luther, and Calvin—a whole calender full of saints. I give God thanks for them, and bare my brow, and do them reverence, and sit down at their feet to learn what they have to offer. They are but leaves and fruit on the tree of humanity which still goes on leafing, flowering, fruiting with other Isaiahs, and Christs, whereof there is no end.[27]

Parker denies the reality of what traditional religion calls evil. Since the universe has been perfectly created by a perfect and benevolent God, evil must be non-existent. His argument in this regard follows closely that of the deists and transcendentalists. Parker objects to the notion in the Bible that "God repents having made mankind" when he saw what sinful creatures they have become. Historical religions have deeply erred in asserting an evil principle to exist in man and the creation. Even though theologians talk about the infinite goodness of God and the perfection of his providence,

> they have yet a certain belief in a devil; even if it is not always a personal devil, at any rate it is a principle of absolute evil, which, they fear will somehow outwit and override God, getting possession of the world.[28]

Parker blames the existence of this doctrine on the "dark notion of God which haunts the theology of Christendom, of the Hebrew, Mohametan, and Hindu world." For example, the popular Calvinistic theology "sees the evil principle . . . in the insects which infect the fruit trees and grain of New England," forgetting that God cares for those insects as well as man. When we study more profoundly, "we see there is no evil principle, but a good principle, so often misunderstood by men." If we begin with the concept of the Infinite God, "we know the purpose is good before we comprehend the means thereto."[29] Parker repeats the deist's argument that "partial evil is universal good," when he writes:

> God made the world in such manner that these partial evils would take place; and they take place with his infinite knowledge, and under His infinite providence. So when we see these evils, we know that though immense, they are partial evils compensated by constants somewhere, and provided for in the infinite engineering of God, so that they shall be the cause of some ultimate good. For mankind has a right to be perfectly created from perfect motives, for a perfect purpose, of perfect material, and with the means to achieve that purpose. . . . His hand is indorsed on each race, each family, each tribe, each nation of mankind. You cannot suppose—as writers of the Old Testament do—that the affairs of the world look desperate to God, and He repents having made mankind, or any fraction of the human race.[30]

In another passage Parker refers to nature as belying the fact that God is "malignant and capricious." He substantiates his point by enumerating the beauty and perfection of specific forms in nature. One is reminded of Whitman's lyrical flights, and of his almost inexhaustible catalogues.

> Look up at the stars, study the mathematics of the heavens writ in those gorgeous diagrams of fire where all is law, order, harmony, beauty without end; look down on the ant hills in the fields some morning in early summer, study the ethics of the emmets, all law, order, harmony, beauty without end; look round on the cattle, on the birds, on the cold

fishes in the stream, the reptiles, insects and see the mathematics of their structure, and the ethics of their lives; do you find any sign that the first person of the Godhead is malignant or capricious, and the fourth person thereof is a devil; that hate preponderates in the world?[31]

In asserting that the universe is moral, Parker makes use of an argument that Emerson was to develop further in his idea of "Compensation." Like Emerson, Parker felt that there was an equilibrium or balance of forces throughout nature. God, he says, foresaw all the upheavals and tragedies in nature and human society, and counterbalanced them with propitious and benevolent events. When science discovered some little "perturbations" or spots on the sun, timid men feared that "the earth will fall into the fire and the world be burned up." After awhile we find that these "perturbations" disturb only the astronomer who is doubtful of God; "to the Cause and Providence of the world they were eternally known; forecared for, that they are normal acts of faithful matter." And so uninterrupted from its unswerving course

the world rolls on. Constant is balanced by constant. Variable holds variable in check. In her cyclic rotation round the earth, the moon nods; the earth oscillates in her rhythmic round, while the sun nods also, as the center of gravity of the solar system shifts now a little this way, then a little that; nay, the whole solar system it is likely, swings a little from side to side; but all this has been foreseen, provided for, balanced by forces which never sleep, and one thing set over against another in such a sort that all work together for good, and the great chariot of matter sweeps on through starry space keeping its God appointed track. Such is the providence of God in the universe, not an atom of star-dust is lost out of the sky; . . . such are the laws by which God works His functions out in nature.[32]

In his impassioned utterances on the glory and perfection of man and nature, Parker comes close to the concept of the divinity of man found in Emerson and Whitman, indeed in the transcendentalists generally. He is not quite prepared to assert, as unreservedly as they, that man is divine and that he can become God, in Emerson's terms, during those moments of deepest insight when the Oversoul flows through him. Parker is closer to the deists in his natural religion; he is still a rationalist and makes use of essentially deistic arguments. He does, however, show transcendental leanings when he says that intuition is an alternate path to the true religion of nature. It is "only gradually that we approach to the true system of nature by observation and reasoning. . . ." But by another direction we can reach the same goal:

> if we are faithful, the great truths of morality and religion, the deep sentiment of love of man and love of God, are perceived intuitively, and by instinct as it were, though our theology be imperfect and miserable.[33]

Parker sought to purify traditional Christianity of its harsh and narrow doctrines, and enlarge its scope to include "new knowledge," but especially to rid it of hypocrisy and false piety. He longed for the same spirit that spoke through "Isaiah's hallowed lips" and the simple and uncorrupted morality of Jesus, the permanent and eternal truths of the tradition without the false supernatural trappings. It is the latter which "must perish." "The trouble with revealed religion," says Parker, "is that man goes to church the first day of the week, and is a sinner on the other six. He communes with God through bread and wine and refuses to commune with Him in buying and selling, is a liar and a usurer . . . before men, while he professes to be a saint before God. What is taught to him as revealed religion does not rebuke his pride nor correct his conduct. . . . Hitherto forms of religion have been a wedge to sever and not a tie to bind." Therefore Parker enjoins:

> the function of the Church will be to keep all the old which is good, and get all the possible good which is new. No creed, no history, or Bible shall interpose a cloud betwixt man and God: reverence for Moses, Jesus, or Mohamet shall no more be a stone between our eyes and truth, but a glass

telescope, a microscope to bring the thought of God yet nearer to our hearts. The Bible's letter shall no longer kill; but the spirit which "touched Isaiah's hallowed lips with fire" and flamed in the life of a Nazarene carpenter till its light shone round the world, will dwell also in many a new-born soul. No man shall be a master, to rule with authority over our necks; but whoso can teach shall be our friend and guide to help us on the heavenly road.[34]

Like his fellow believers in natural religion, Parker looks to the future for the realization of his vision. Not only the high moral sentiments within the historical faiths are needed, but a broader, more inclusive religious attitude brought about by the "new" knowledge that shows nature to be the revelation of God.

The whole world will be a Temple, every spot holy ground, every bush burning with the Infinite; all time the Lord's day, and every moral act worship and a sacrament . . . then men will see that fraud in work and in trade is a sin; that no orthodoxy of belief, no multitudinous prayers, no bodily presence in a meeting house, no acceptance of a sacrament can ever atone for neglect of the great natural sacrament which God demands of everyman.[35]

And furthermore, this religion of the future must be universal, and "take on a general human form." Parker's transcendentalism reveals itself most glowingly in the peroration of "Theism, Atheism and The Popular Theology," in which he envisions a one world unity of the human family, a theme which Whitman was to take up and glorify.

This religion must take a cosmic, or general human form, in the life of mankind. It will unite all nations into one great bond of brotherhood . . . with personal unity for all, but individual freedom for each; as several persons are joined together in a family. . . . as the families form a community, and the communities a state, with social and national unity of action; so the nations of the world will join together, all working with cosmic human unity of action, but each having its own national individuality of action. . . .

Then law would be justice, loyalty righteousness, and patriotism humanity. Men conscious of the same human nature, and consciously serving the Infinite God, must needs find their religion transcending the bounds of their family, community, church, and nation, and reaching out to every human soul.[36]

CHAPTER SIX

Ralph Waldo Emerson

In the writings of Ralph Waldo Emerson natural religion reaches its fullest transcendental expression. Although Parker leaned toward an intuitive philosophy of religion, as discussed previously, he did not develop his thought along those lines to the extent that Emerson did. Like Parker, Emerson was highly critical of the "pale negations" of Boston Unitarianism; but he did not rest content there, but took to the lecture platform, where he expounded his special brand of spiritual individualism and the doctrine of the Oversoul.

Emerson placed himself in the center of the Universe—and from that vantage point the Oversoul was seen and felt to be the spiritual force pervading man and nature. Man needed no church, no priests, no set of doctrines to be taken on faith. He alone, in the deepest recesses of his soul, through intuitive perception, experienced the oneness of man, God and nature. Emerson considered the supernatural elements (miracles, dogmas, revelation) within Christianity to be irrelevant and an impediment to the soul's understanding of itself. In addition, Emerson and the transcendentalists strongly attacked the Lockian epistemology upon which the current Unitarian theology was based. They looked to the German Romantic philosophers: Kant, Fichte and Schelling, and to Coleridge for a deeper understanding of the truths of religion.

Transcendentalism, although it attacked rationalism, nevertheless did not repudiate the essential position of the deists in
regard to historical Christianity, or regarding nature as the
means by which man understood God. They adhered to virtually
all the points that the deists had made; (1) belief in a benevolent
Deity, (2) the universe operating according to unswerving
natural law, (3) the goodness of man because he was created
by a perfect Deity, and (4) nature as a reflection of the Divine
Mind. The difference between the transcendentalists and the
deists over the limitation of reason, therefore, was a difference
of methodology not conviction. In varying degrees (Emerson
and Jones Very being probably the most extreme examples),
the transcendentalists claimed that instinct and intuition were
superior paths to divine truths—superior specifically to what
they felt were the logical abstractions and limited scope of
Christian theologies. Indeed, Emerson in his Journal referred
to all theology as the "mumps and measles of the soul."[1] The
individual, he felt, has all he needs within him to realize the
nature of religious truths. The criticism was unyielding. The
1830's marked the beginning of the spiritual and cultural
emancipation of American writers and thinkers, and ushered in
the richest period in our national literature.

What the transcendentalists achieved in regard to the development of natural religion was to imbue deism with a more
emotional and mystical quality. God was no longer the force
that started the universe in motion and then took no further
interest in human affairs; rather God was conceived as existing
within man and nature (immanent), as well as extending above
and beyond the whole creation (transcendent). There was no
boundary between spirit and matter, mind and body—in a word,
the old Christian dualism was attacked as being erroneous. The
transcendentalists sought unity which was to be achieved by the
individual perceiving his soul to be one with the Oversoul.

Transcendentalism did not spring full-grown from the head
of the Concord seer, but it took years of hard reflection and
soul-searching before the germinal ideas matured into the famous
concepts of the Oversoul, compensation, and the divinity of

man. Emerson's *Journals* chart the growth of his mind from the early doubts and disillusionment with his inherited Calvinism and Unitarianism to the latter all-embracing philosophy. Thus they reflect a good deal of the history of New England religious thought from Calvinism to Unitarianism to transcendentalism. How far Emerson traveled from his early jottings in his Journal is illustrated by the following excerpt dated April 16, 1862:

> There can be no question that from both the poles to the Equator, under every sun, man will be found selfish, comparatively indifferent to the general welfare whenever it is put in competition with private interest.... war is waged in the Universe without true end, between Virtue and Vice; they are light and darkness, they cannot harmonize. Upon earth they are forcibly consorted, and the perpetual struggle which they make, separate by distinct line man from throughout the world.[2]

As his thought developed, Emerson became increasingly critical of historical Christianity. Like the deists before him, he attacked its supernatural elements: the divinity of Christ, the Bible as revelation; indeed he attacked Christian revelation because he felt it denied the universal truth of God to all people and restricted it to one group.

In 1832 Emerson preached a sermon on *The Lord's Supper* before the congregation of the Second Church of Boston. In the preceding June he had asked the Church proprietors for permission to discontinue administering the sacrament of communion according to the accepted ritual. In this carefully thought-out sermon, he expressed the reasons why he could not conscientiously observe the communion. His main point was that Jesus did not intend the ritual to be performed century after century. After considerable discussion the members of the Church committee could not agree to Emerson's request. His resignation as minister was accepted, though with regret.[3] Throughout the address Emerson spoke in a tone that was to be his central emphasis: the individual needs no mediator between himself and God. Emerson criticized the undue stress placed on the person of Christ in contrast to his spiritual importance.

I fear it is the effect of this ordinance to clothe Jesus with an authority which he never claimed, and which distracts the mind of the worshipper. I know our opinions differ much respecting the nature and offices of Christ, and to the degree of veneration to which he is entitled. I am so much a Unitarian as this: that I believe the human mind can admit one God, and that every effort to pay religious homage to more than one Being goes to take away all right ideas. I appeal, brethren, to your individual experience. In the moment that you make the least petition to God, though it be but a silent wish that He may approve you, or add one moment to your life—do you not, in the very act, necessarily exclude all other beings from your thought? In this act, the soul stands alone with God, and Jesus is no more present to your mind than your brother or your child.[4]

His *Journals* record other criticisms and doubts as to the truth of Christian revelation, and indeed all religious creeds in general. The following is dated 1826:

What security is there that there are more genuine creeds than those that went before, or that another age may not treat them with the same irreverence?[5]

He records his dissatisfaction with the doctrines of Calvinism, specifically their ineffectiveness in morally elevating the individual.

People would teach me what they think concerning modes of Justification, and how their supposed offices of Christ are compatible with the Father's dignity, etc. Will they teach me how to resist my temptations? Will they teach me how to be a good man? I have nothing to do with their creeds. It is more than I can do to keep the commandments.[6]

Further along in the Journal he notes the hypocrisy and lack of love at the bottom of formal religion. Love was the creative force in these religions, he thought; they were the heart's work "But those fervent generations passed away, things went downward and the forms remain, but the soul is well-nigh gone," Calvinism stands, he fears, "by pride and ignorance; and

Unitarianism, as a sect stands by [virtue of] the opposition of
Calvinism."[7] With growing assurance he declaims, "Who can
be a Calvinist, or who an atheist? God has opened this knowledge to us to correct our theology and educate our minds."[8]

The "knowledge" that Emerson referred to was scientific
knowledge. Emerson thought much about the discoveries of
science, and felt that they could not help altering the opinions
of men in regard to religion. At this early period in his development he finds it impossible to reconcile the Calvinistic scheme
for salvation with the Copernican view of the universe. He notes
that Newton through his study of astronomy and his discovery
of the laws of motion was driven to relinquish his former beliefs and become a Unitarian. Laplace, on the other hand, who
lived in a Catholic country, became an infidel and substituted
necessity for God.[9] Emerson, at one time, even approved Paley's[10]
analogy of the world-machine, because it was an early attempt
to extend Newtonian physics to morals. Of course, he realized
the spiritual inadequacies of a watchlike universe, advocated
by Paley and the other deists, which like the science that
"murders to dissect," abolished the miracle of life or creation
by removing the necessary presence of God. He was not opposed
to "science *per se,* but to science which had forgotten the
poetry of ideas in the assurance that the sensible fact was
sufficient, and that the accumulation would give meaning. And
he was not so much opposed to Paley's analogy as analogy, but
to its implications of determinism."[11] However, when its empirical findings were wedded to Emerson's unique transcendentalism, it would widen man's spiritual and religious understanding.
In his recollection of the transcendental movement, Emerson,
later in life, said the following about the influence of science
upon religious thought:

> But I think the paramount source of the religious revolu-
> tion was Modern Science: beginning with Copernicus, who
> destroyed the pagan fictions of the Church, by showing
> mankind that the earth on which we live was not the center
> of the Universe, . . . Astronomy taught us our insignificance
> in Nature; showed that our sacred as our profane history

had been written in gross ignorance of the laws, which were far grander than we knew; and compiled a certain extension and uplifting of our views of the Deity and his Providence. This correction of our superstitions was confirmed by the new science of Geology, and the whole train of discoveries in every department. But we presently saw also that the religious nature in man was not affected by these errors in his understanding. The religious sentiment made nothing of bulk or size, or far or near; triumphed over time as well as space, humility, or charity, which the old ignorant saints had taught him, was still forever true.[12]

After his resignation as minister in the Unitarian Church, Emerson sailed for Europe. His mind was filled with doubt and uncertainty; he wanted to confirm the feelings and intuitions he speaks of in his Journals. He longed to meet living writers— Carlyle, Coleridge, Wordsworth, Landor—and by talking with them hoped to gain a new perspective. While traveling on the continent, he was deeply struck by the beauty of the Italian cities, and spoke glowingly of their cathedrals and of the statues of Michelangelo. The latter's "Moses" filled him with awe, leading him to term it "the Jewish Law embodied in a Man." In the zoological gardens at Paris, he underwent a strange spiritual experience that proved to be the greatest lesson of his travels. "Observing the rocks, the grass, the fishes, the insects, the lions, vultures, and elephants, he felt a conviction stirring in him that these forms of life expressed some property in himself." He had had similar experiences in the woods at home. He felt a kindred nature with all these creatures. Nature was felt to be a living whole; everywhere the Divine Mind manifested itself. "He was struck by Lamarck's ideas—men would rise above their conventional notions, emerge from their belief in mere prescriptions."[13]

However, the trip as a whole failed of its intended purpose. He was disappointed with the men whom he met insofar as he hoped to learn anything about religion from them. "Carlyle," he says, writing in his Journals on the way home, "almost grudges the poor peasant his Calvinism." Emerson notes that although he has practical personal difficulties, he for one would not discourage the scrupulous religious observances of the masses. But philosophically he believes that the error of religionists lies in the fact that "they do not know the extent of the harmony or the depth of their moral nature; that they are clinging to little positive, verbal, formal versions of the moral law, and very imperfect versions too, while the infinite laws, the laws of Law, the great circling truths whose only adequate symbol is the material laws, the astronomy, etc., are all unobserved and sneered at when spoken of as frigid and insufficient." He calls Calvinism such an "imperfect version of the Moral Law." Unitarianism is another, and every sect of Christian and pagan faith taught by incapable teachers is such a version. On the other hand, under the leadership of true teachers, the falsehoods, the narrowness, the sectarianisms of each disappear, "and the sublimity and the depth of the Original is penetrated and exhibited to men."[14] In addition, all that appeals in these established systems to men "is so much of the Moral Truth as is in them, and by the instructive selection of the preacher is made to shine forth when the system is assailed." And because of this "One Bottom," he says, the eminent men of every church, Socrates, Thomas à Kempis, Fénelon, Butler, Penn, Swedenborg, Channing, expound the same ideas.[15]

Emerson, as an afterthought to his reflections on the limitations of institutional religion, hits upon the theme he was constantly to reiterate during his lifetime.

A man contains all that is needful to his government within himself. He is made a law unto himself. All real good or evil that can befall him must be from himself. . . . Nothing can be given to him or taken from him but always there is a compensation. There is a correspondence between the human soul and everything that exists in the world; more properly everything that is known to man. Instead of studying things without the principles of them, all may be penetrated into within him. Every act puts the agent in a new condition. The purpose of life seems to be to acquaint a man with himself. He is not to live to the future as described to him, but to live to the real future by living to the real present. The highest revelation is that God is in every man.[16]

On his way home from Europe in the fall of 1833, when asked what he meant by morals, his only reply was, "I cannot define, and care not to define. It is man's business to observe, and the definition of moral nature must be the slow result of years, of lives of states, perhaps being." But he was very much aware of the direction in which his inner experience pointed.

> Milton describes himself in his letter to Diodati as enamored of moral perfection. He did not love it more than I. That which I cannot yet declare has been my angel from childhood until now ... What is this they say about wanting mathematical certainty for moral truths? I have always affirmed they had it. Yet they ask me whether I know the soul immortal. No. But I do not know the how to be eternal. I believe in this life."[17]

Christianity, he maintains, has become formal and cold, and no one dare teach essential truth for "fear of shocking." He believes truth to be self-evident, self-subsisted, and primary to life and teaching of Jesus. He protests being told to be humble because of the injunction of Jesus—whom he is told God sent. "But how do I know God sent him? Because your own heart teaches the same things he taught? Why then shall I not go to my heart first?"[18]

In October of 1833, Emerson reflects further upon Christianity and the nature of Christ. Here again the same criticism, though more explicit, is made against an undue glorification of Christ, that he discussed in his sermon on the *Lord's Supper*.

> It seems to me that the perspective of time as it sets everything in the right point of view, does the same by Christianity. We learn to look at it now as a part of the history of the world, to see how it rests in the broad basis of man's moral nature, and is not itself that basis. I cannot but think that Jesus Christ will be better loved by being less adored. He has had an unnatural, an artificial place for ages in human opinion—a place too high for love. There is

a recoil of affections from all authority and force... Now
that the scriptures are read with purged eyes, it is seen that
he is only to be loved for so much goodness and wisdom
as was in him, which are the only things for which a sound
human mind can love any person....

But will not this come to be thought the chief value of
his teaching, that is, of Christianity, to wit, that it was a
great stand for man's spiritual nature against the sensual-
ism, the forms, the crimes of the age in which he appeared
and those that preceded it.

The things that he said—must be looked upon as one
affirmation, proclamation glorious of moral truth, but not
as the last affirmation. There shall be a thousand more.[19]

Emerson claims it would be very inconsistent to set bounds
upon a soul possessed of such love as he advocates above; none
knew better than Christ that every soul occupies a new position,
"and that if the stars cannot be counted, nor the sands of the
sea, neither can those moral truths be numbered and ended of
which the material creation is only a shadow."[20]

It is apparent from these quotations that Emerson's resignation from the pulpit of the Second Church of Boston was due
not only to a disagreement over the performance of a sacrament,
but rather to a fundamental difference that strikes at the roots
of traditional Christianity. Like the deists, Emerson denied
Christian revelation and the divinity of Christ. What he spoke
for most strongly was individual freedom as opposed to authority
in religion. Emerson, at this point, felt himself to be within the
ken of his inherited religion, but he was honest enough to
realize the danger of such a stand. "I know very well," he wrote
in his Journal, "that it is a bad sign in a man to be too con-
scientious, and stick at gnats. The most desperate scoundrels
have been the overrefiners. Without accommodation society is
impractical." But, he adds, it is not right for him to go to an
institution which is esteemed holiest by the members of the
community, with indifference and dislike. His final words are,
"This is the end of my opposition, I am not interested in it."[21]
He undoubtedly felt disappointed and sorrowful at the time,
but the inner man was ready to take on the higher duty of

proclaiming a living religion in the divinity of man. He took to the lecture platform at the Boston Lyceum, a newly organized movement for adult education. At the East Lexington Church, where he preached after resigning from the Second Church, he gave many talks that he had delivered previously in his lecture courses in Boston. In later years Emerson said that it seemed "strange" that the same people will gladly hear and accept certain truths when delivered from the lecture platform which they will not tolerate from the pulpit.[22]

In order to grasp fully the essence of the conflict between transcendentalism and Unitarianism, it is necessary to point out the philosophical differences they held regarding reason and intuition. Dissatisfied with the shallow rationalistic theology of the Boston Divinity School the young transcendentalists read avidly the works of Kant, Coleridge, Schelling, Fichte, writers who asserted the validity of innate ideas and opposed the English empirical thinkers from Locke to Hume. Early in his Journal, Emerson indicated his dissatisfaction with empiricism, and the need to derive a new epistemology with which to better formulate his still amorphous thought.

> Mr. Hume's Essay upon Necessary Connection proves that events are conjoined, and not connected; that we have no knowledge but from experience. We have no experience of a Creator and therefore know of none. The constant appeal is to our feelings from the glazed lies of the deceived, but one would feel safer and prouder to see the victorious answer to these calumnies upon our nature set down in impregnable propositions.[23]

Later on Emerson referred to empiricism as the "linear logic," and for him it conveyed this sense of the despair of the times. "A new disease has fallen on the life of man ... our torment is Unbelief, the Uncertainty as to what we ought to do; the distrust of the value of what we do, and the distrust that the Necessity (which we all at last believe in) is fair and beneficient. Our religion assumes the negative form of rejection."[24]

The linear logic, then, in a large measure, was responsible for the decline in conviction and faith. It could not affirm.

It was limited to the senses and to the surface of things. Emerson and the transcendentalists would probe deeper and broader, beyond sense, beyond phenomena visible to the eye. Emerson sought to unfold a new way to reality and revitalize religion, now sterile and dry, based as it was on an epistemology limited to the passive reception of sensations.

"For, unless the mind contributed something to perception beyond its machinelike manipulations—and the mind, Hume had shown had no necessary assurance that the sensations it put together revealed the actual but unknowable relations of the universe—the mind received only an impression of surface: the self found itself outside the universe."[25]

If one sought the common-sense answer, believing that in the act of perception he actually experienced a real objective world, he was still limited to surface. The consequence of this Lockian epistemology was that one still perceived only the material world of secondary causes, and the problem of meaning of the self was not answered. "To follow Lockian sensationalism was to reduce the universe to one dimension—that, as Whitehead said, of 'one-eyed reason deficient in its vision of depth.' "[26]

The problem, then, that Emerson was confronted with was the erecting of a vertical standard of value perpendicular to the enslaving horizontal logic of his time. The horizontal line represents "the ground line of familiar facts," the one-dimensional world of fact, of space, time and history, a universe reduced to the experience of the senses. It gives us, to use the transcendental word which distinguishes between the superficially outward and the meaningful inner—only the world's *surface.* "We dwell amidst surfaces," Emerson wrote, "and surface laps so closely on surface that we cannot easily pierce to see the interior organism." Again: "It is the depth at which we live, and not all the surface extension, that imports. We piece to the eternity, of which time is the flitting surface." Looking out of the inner eye, he said: "How does everybody live on the outside of the world!"[27] The vertical axis gave the universe its spiritual dimension; it gave scope to the mythic, symbolic, and religious components of human experience. "The vertical was the inner and spiritual and 'put nature underfoot' by making nature serve the moral needs of man."[28]

Thus Emerson's reading of Coleridge, Kant, and the German transcendental philosophers gave him the needed epistemology with which to express his vision. He borrowed the Coleridgian (derived from Kant) distinction between reason and understanding. Reason operated along the vertical axis, understanding along the horizontal world of fact. Reason transcended sense impressions and gazes upon the eternal reality; understanding was bound to the immediate and mundane. The following excerpt is taken from a letter written to his brother Edward, dated 1834.

Reason is the highest faculty of the soul—what we mean often by the soul itself; it never *reasons*, never proves, it simply perceives, it is a vision. The Understanding toils all the time, compares, contrives, adds, argues, near-sighted, but strong-sighted, dwelling in the present, the expedient, the customary. Beasts have some understanding but no Reason. Reason is potentially perfect in every man—Understanding in very different degrees of strength. The thoughts of youth and "first thoughts" are the revelations of Reason, the love of the Beautiful and of Goodness as the highest beauty, the belief in the absolute and universal superiority of the Right and the True. But Understanding that wrinkled calculator, the steward of our house to whom is commited the support of our animal life contradicts evermore these affirmations of Reason and points at Custom and Interest and persuades one that declarations of Reason are false, and another that they are at least impracticable. Yet by and by after having denied our master we come back to see at the end of years, or of life he was the Truth. . . . Religion, Poetry, Honor belong to the Reason, to the real, to the absolute.[29]

In 1836 Emerson published *Nature,* his first book. It represents Emerson's formal expression of the ideas set down piecemeal in his Journal. When he asks those leading questions at the beginning of the essay, "Why should not we also enjoy an original relation to the universe? Why should not we have a poetry and a philosophy of insight and not tradition, and a religion by revelation to us and not the history of [previous revelations]," he was preparing for the subsequent presentation of his new method. The chief idea it developed was the use of nature as the mediating agency between man and God. Emerson asserted that there was an occult relationship between man and nature by which man attains insight and moral growth. We come to understand that relationship, and here Emerson departs from deism, not through studying the details of natural history alone, but by the higher perception of imagination and intuition. Nature educates us morally, both through understanding and reason. "The Understanding adds, divides, combines, measures, and finds nutriment and room for its activity. . . . Reason transfers all these lessons into its own world of thought, by perceiving the analogy that marries Matter and Mind."[30]

The greatest delight which the fields and woods minister is suggestion of an occult relation between man and the vegetable. I am not alone and unacknowledged. They nod to me, and I to them. The waving of the boughs in the storm is new to me and old. It takes me by surprise, and yet is not unknown. Its effect is like that of a higher thought or a better emotion coming over me, when I deemed I was thinking justly or doing right. . . . Standing on the bare ground— my head bathed by the blithe air and uplifted into infinite space—all mean egotism vanishes. I become a transparent eyeball; I am nothing; I see all; the currents of the Universal Being circulate through me; I am part or parcel of God.[31]

Emerson asserted the superiority of vision, because for him it was the only way to "lop off all superficiality and tradition, and fall back on the nature of things."[32] The unity he expounded was actualized by the assumption of a correspondence of the natural and spiritual worlds: "but this correspondence, if it were to fulfill its promise of moral certainty in the conduct of life, had to be renewed daily in man's dynamic experience of self-consciousness."[33] Man, to affirm this unity, took a central position in nature, where in presence of the flux of sensations he felt the informing unity in those moments of deepest inspiration. "The guarantee of the connection of the moral and spiritual worlds was, then, the experience of one's perception of the spirit in the mind and in and behind nature." As the possessor of the intuitive faculty, man was necessarily, in Emerson's view, the center of unity.[34]

And what is most important, not only is the poet or religious genius able to perceive this unity; all men are potentially able to recognize it. Indeed, even in his essay *Nature*, Emerson still made attacks on a religion based on the authority of the few.

> This relation between the mind and matter is not fancied by some poet, but stands in the will of God, and so is free to be known by all men. It appears to men or it does not appear. When in fortunate hours we ponder this miracle, the wise man doubts if at all other times he is not blind and deaf; ... for the Universe becomes transparent, and the light of higher laws than its own shines through it.[35]

The rehabilitation of nature as more than a field of empirical observation led to nature's highest discipline—belief in idealism. "Idealism," Emerson wrote, "is a hypothesis to account for nature by other principles than those of carpentry or chemistry."[36] Its advantage over other methods "is this, that it presents the world in precisely that view which is most desirable to the mind."[37] "Grant us the ideal theory," he wrote, "and the universe is solved. Otherwise, the moment a man discovers that he has aims which his faculties cannot answer, the world becomes a riddle."[38] And even though the denial of the existence of matter haunted Emerson, he found idealism useful because it indicated the dualism of the soul and the world.[39] This dualism was necessary even for a seeker after unity, if God as the absolute ground of being were to be made the unifying force who made the laws of nature reflect the self-evident ideas He planted in the mind of man.

> If Nature is a sufficient account of that Appearance we call the World, that God will teach a human mind, and so make it the receiver of a certain number of congruent sensations, which we call sun, and moon, man and woman, house and

trade ... the noblest ministry of nature is to stand as the apparition of God. It is the organ through which the universal spirit speaks to the individual, and strives to lead back the individual to it.[40]

Nature thus would not be the barrier it remained in Unitarian theology, but could serve man in his search for the living God. Confronting nature in this religious perspective, man would no longer be happy with responding to her merely with his senses, but instead would stand before her feeling her to be "the expositor of the divine mind," perceiving analogies between her phenomena and his thoughts, knowing that they were manifestations of the divine unity. If the material world were the counterpart of the ideal, then "the axioms of physics translate the laws of ethics."[41] "The world is emblematic," Emerson wrote,

Parts of speech are metaphors, because the whole of nature is a metaphor of the human mind. The laws of moral nature answer to those of matter as face to face in a glass. ... A fact is the end or last issue of spirit. The visible creation is the terminus or circumference of the invisible.[42]

Thus armed with his now well-formulated philosophy, Emerson prescribes in confident terms the remedy for his times. Man is at present slumbering spiritually, because "we distrust and deny inwardly our sympathy with nature. We own and disown our relation to it, by turns. We are like Nebuchadnezzar, dethroned, bereft of reason, and eating grass like an ox." "Who," he asks in criticism of the current Unitarianism, "can set limits to the remedial force of spirit?"[43]

At present, man applies to nature but half his force. He works on the world with his understanding alone. ... The problem of restoring to the world original and eternal beauty is solved by the redemption of the soul. The ruin or blank that we see when we look at nature, is in our own eye. The axis of vision is not coincident with the axis of things, and so they appear not transparent, but opaque. The reason why the world lacks unity, and lies broken in heaps, is because man is disunited with himself. He cannot be a naturalist until he satisfies all the demands of the spirit. Love is as much a demand as perception. Indeed, neither can be perfect without the other. In the uttermost meaning of the words, thought is devout, and devotion is thought. Deep calls unto deep. But in actual life, the marriage is not celebrated. There are innocent men who worship God after the tradition of their fathers, but their sense of duty has not yet extended to the use of all their faculties. And there are patient naturalists, but they freeze their subject under the wintry light of understanding. Is not prayer also a study of truth—a sally of the soul into the unfound infinite? No man ever prayed heartily without learning something. But when a faithful thinker, resolute to detach every object from personal relations and see it in the light of thought, shall at the same time kindle science with the fire of the holiest affections, then will God go forth anew into the creation.[44]

The reference to "men who worship God after the tradition of their fathers" undoubtedly was a gentle jibe aimed at the Unitarian elders. But Emerson was to make assertions and criticisms of a stronger nature. In the "Divinity School Address," given before the graduating class of the Harvard Divinity School, Emerson openly attacked the supernatural basis of Christianity within the citadel of Unitarianism itself. Let man worship God without "mediator or veil"; there would be no need for a church or a priesthood, intoned Emerson. The address was found to be so incendiary that thirty years were to pass before Emerson was to be allowed to speak at Harvard again. Another result of the address was that it opened up the pamphlet war between the Unitarians and their young wayward charges, the transcendentalists. There was much smoke, and the language used was strong indeed for these mild, rational men. But, if anything, the controversy (reminiscent of another, incidentally, waged a generation earlier between the Calvinists and the Unitarians) succeeded in more sharply delineating the differences between transcendentalism and historical Christianity. Emerson's main point was that Christianity had become lifeless and frigid;

ministers treated religion as if it were over and done with. "It is the office of the true teacher," said Emerson, "to show that God is, not was."[45]

Historical Christianity has "fallen into the error that corrupts all attempts to communicate religion." It is not a doctrine of the soul, but limits itself to the personal and the ritual. "It has dwelt, it dwells, with noxious exaggeration about the *person* of Jesus. The soul knows no person. It invites every man to expand to the full circle of the universe, and will have no preferences but those of spontaneous love."[46] Another defect of the traditional way, and "a consequence of the first," is that it speaks of religion as something given in the past and not a living vital principle. "The Moral Nature, that Law of laws, whose revelations introduce greatness—yea, God himself—into the open soul, is not explored as the fountainhead of the established teaching in society." Men have come to think that the revelation is over and done with, "as if God were dead." This inhibits faith, by restricting the preacher, and thus the best of institutions becomes inadequate and ineffective. Directing himself to the young ministers, Emerson exhorts them to look upon their office as "the first in the world." The term "revelation," is not to be taken in the traditional sense—like Theodore Parker, Emerson meant a natural revelation, of the truths of the soul speaking through each man in those moments of deepest spiritual insight. It is due to precisely the lack of this vital element that faith is receding.

> The time is coming when all men will see that the gift of God to the soul is not a vaunting, overpowering, excluding sanctity, but a sweet natural goodness . . . And it is my duty to say to you that the need was never greater of new revelation than now.[47]

Emerson then offers his suggestions to remedy the defect of current religion. "The remedy," he says, "is already declared in the ground of our complaint of the Church. We have contrasted the Church with the Soul. In the soul then, let the redemption be sought." Man makes all books understandable, makes things transparent, makes all religions and forms. "He is religious. Man is the wonderworker. He is seen amid miracles."[48]

> The stationariness of religion; the assumption that the age of inspiration is past, that the Bible is closed; the fear of degrading the character of Jesus by representing him as a man; indicate with sufficient clearness the falsehood of our theology. . . . The true Christianity—a faith like Christ's in the infinitude of men—is lost. None believeth in the soul of man, but only in some man or person old or departed. Ah, me! no man goeth alone. All men go in flocks to this saint or that poet, avoiding the God who seeth in secret. . . . Once leave your own knowledge of God, your sentiment, and take secondary knowledge, as St. Paul's or George Fox's, or Swedenborg's, and you get wide from God with every year this secondary form lasts, and if, as now, for centuries—the chasm yawns to that breadth, that men can scarcely be convinced there is in them anything divine.[49]

Emerson insisted that the only way to experience God is through the private, inward vision; all the rituals, theologies, articles of belief of the traditional religious are an impediment to the soul. "Let me admonish you," he said, "first of all to go alone: to refuse the good models, even those which are sacred in the imagination of men, and dare to love God without mediator or veil." The imitator can never attain the lofty level of the original model; he falls into mediocrity. Emerson called the young ministers newborn bards of the Holy Ghost. He called upon them to cast behind all conformity, "and acquaint men at first hand with the Deity."[50]

The address naturally caused a furor. A pamphlet controversy ensued between the Unitarians and transcendentalists. Andrews Norton, the head of Harvard Divinity School, delivered a strongly worded address before the Alumni in July of 1839, attacking the points made by Emerson the previous year. Norton was a key figure in the argument over miracles set off by Emerson's volatile doctrines. Norton attempted to prove that the miracles which Emerson made light of were essential to Christianity, that if they were denied nothing was left.[51]

> The latest form of infidelity is distinguished by assuming the Christian name, while it strikes directly at the root of faith in Christianity, and indirectly of all religion, by denying the miracles attesting the divine mission of Christ. ... Christianity was a revelation from God; and, in being so, it was itself a miracle. No proof of His [Christ's] divine commission could be afforded, but through miraculous displays of God's power. Nothing is left that can be called Christianity, if its miraculous character be denied. Its essence is gone; its evidence is annihilated. Its truths, involving the highest interests of man, the facts which it makes known, and which are implied in its very existence as a divine revelation, rest no longer on the authority of God. ... The rejection of historical Christianity is, of course, accompanied by the rejection of all that mass of evidence, which in the view of a Christian established the truth of his religion. This evidence, it is said, consists only of probabilities. We want certainty. The dwellers in the region of shadows complain that the solid earth is not stable enough for them to rest on. They have firm footing in the clouds.[52]

Norton's reply to Emerson indicates the depth of the conflict between natural religion and traditional faith. The traditionalists asserted that religion loses its name when one removes the miraculous elements upon which it is based. Morality then, according to the theologians, no longer rests upon the authority of God, but on human agency. Norton argues that religion requires faith in the God-given authority of the Scriptures. An individual is guilty of the worst blasphemy, as Emerson and believers in natural religion in general were, in denying supernatural revelation. Belief in the divine origin of the Scriptures and the faith of the individual in those who interpret the Scriptures are essential to the existence of Christianity. Norton is highly critical of natural religion in the following quotation. It presumes, he says, to defy the authority of those with whom Christianity is entrusted.

There is, then no mode of establishing religious belief, but by the exercise of reason, by investigation, by forming a probable judgment upon facts. Christianity in requiring this process, requires nothing more than any other form of religion must do. He who on this account rejects it, cannot have recourse to Natural Religion. . . . But we have not, it may be said, yet removed the difficulty, that the evidence and character of Christianity, in order to be properly understood require investigations which are beyond the capacity or the opportunities of a great majority of men. . . . Our belief in those truths, the evidence of which we cannot fully examine ourselves is founded to a greater or lesser degree on the testimony of others, who have examined their evidence, and whom we regard as intelligent and trustworthy . . . this faith in the knowledge of others may be called belief on trust, or belief on authority.[53]

Emerson took little part in the argument over miracles waged between Andrews Norton and his former students at the Divinity School. Of these Orestes A. Brownson and George Ripley were the most outspoken. But Emerson's position on miracles can be clearly traced in his writings. In the "Divinity School Address," speaking about the undue reverence for the divinity of Christ, he says the following:

The idioms of his language and the figures of his rhetoric have usurped the place of his truth; and churches are not built on his principles but on his tropes. Christianity became a Mythus, as the poetic teachings of Greece and Egypt before, . . . The word Miracle, as pronounced by Christian churches, gives a false impression; it is Monster. It is not one with the blowing clover and the falling rain.[54]

Emerson felt that man himself must discover the genuine miracle in his own life, that is, in his relation to the laws of nature. "All our life is a miracle. Ourselves are the greatest wonder of all."[55] Once man has come to recognize the true relation of his life to that of nature, he no longer will find the miracle in an interruption of natural order, but in the moral bond uniting his soul and the Universe. Self-reflection itself became the way "to receive truth immediately from God without any medium."[56] Thus Emerson is very much in the tradition of natural religion in regard to miracles. Ethan Allen, Thomas Paine, and Theodore Parker had renounced miracles as a disruption of the laws of nature. God worked through natural law. The creation and life itself were miracles enough.

Likewise, Emerson's attitude toward the Bible is found to be in agreement with that of the deists. The Bible is not a record of divine dispensation, but a human document which contains great moral and ethical insights, and also a history of a people. What Emerson disliked in the Bible was the stern command of God to man; the "Thou shalts" thundered too strongly for his serene spirit to respond with unquestioning obedience. Emerson shunned a morality based on supernatural fiat; he liked to insist that man can do no wrong if he relied on his true self. Rules of conduct imposed from without would, according to Emerson, defeat their intended purpose because of their merely negative function. Hence he makes the following criticism of the Bible:

It is because the Bible wears black cloth, it comes with a certain official claim against which the mind revolts. The book has its own nobilities—might well be charming, if it were left simply on its own merits, as the others; but this "you must," "it is your duty" repels.[57]

He felt that a great deal that was said about the Bible was grossly superstitious, and he could not be convinced that the New Testament unfolded a plan that had been prophesized in the Old Testament. Although he recognized the surpassing depth of thought in the Bible, he could not regard it in the same light as did historical Christianity. He frankly admitted that he found Marcus Aurelius, or Stanley's *Lives of the Philosophers,* more agreeable than St. Paul or St. John.[58]

When Emerson mentions the Bible in his later writings, he refers not only to the Hebrew Bible, but to the bibles of all peoples. Natural religion was critical of all special revelations to groups of "chosen people" whether they were Christian,

Hebrew, Hindu, Mohammedan, etc.[59] References are therefore
made to the Bhagavad-Gita, Upanishads, Koran, the Chinese
classics. Emerson and the transcendentalists perceived the unifying principle underlying all these great expressions of spirituality.
They ignored the rituals and creeds of these various religions
and sought to bring them together in one grand vision, a theme
which Whitman later was to thread throughout his *Leaves of
Grass.* Emerson called upon each man to make his own Bible,
to gather from his reading of Shakespeare, Seneca, Moses, John,
Paul, those words and sentences that came like a "blast of
triumph." Later, at the age of forty, he hoped for a new Bible
that "should open the history of the planet and bind all
tendencies and dwarf all the Epics and Philosophies we have. It
will have no book of Ruth and Esther, no Song of Solomon,
nor excellent sophistical Pauls."[60] In July, 1842, while editing
the "Ethical Scriptures" for *Dial,* Emerson wrote the following
in his introduction:

> We commence in the present number the printing of a series
> of selections from the oldest ethical and religious writings
> of men, exclusive of the Hebrew and the Greek Scriptures.
> Each nation has its bible more or less pure; none has yet
> been willing or able in a wise and devout spirit to collate
> its own with those of other nations, and sinking the civil-
> historical and ritual portions to bring together the grand
> expressions of the moral sentiment in different ages and
> races, the rules for the guidance of life, the bursts of piety
> and of abandonment to the Invisible and Eternal; a work
> inevitable sooner or later, and which we hope is to be done
> by religion and not by literature.[61]

There are two concepts which must still be discussed if one
is fully to grasp the nature of Emerson's differences with
historical Christianity and his similarities to the deists. These
two concepts are the meaning of evil and retribution for sins.

Much has been written on the subject; many critics say
Emerson avoided the problem of evil, and thus vitiated his
philosophy by excluding it from his scheme. This is not entirely
accurate. Emerson regarded evil negatively; that is, for him,

evil was the absence of good.[62] Therefore, it was not a real or blighting force as it is within Christianity. Satan and his legions fill up Christian theology. He is the personification of evil, and man must be constantly on his guard to avoid his snares and pitfalls. The world is regarded as a stage where God and Satan engage in eternal conflict for the soul of man, who struggles, with the aid of moral inculcation of priests and ministers, to gain his cherished goal—a future abode in heaven. If he failed in the struggle, or if God willed, or predestined it, he wound up in the fiery pit of hell. Even though the Unitarians renounced a great deal of the bleakness and terror of Calvinism, and no longer believed in predestination, they nevertheless held to the doctrine of future reward and punishment, and a belief in the reality of evil. Emerson departs from his inherited religion on both these points.

Emerson's view of evil is similar to that of the mystics who regard evil, in the larger sense as illusory. They do not deny the existence of individual evils, such as, pain, disease, misfortunes. Experience of these evils my enlarge the individual's experience and knowledge of the world. Emerson suffered from tuberculosis in his youth, and in St. Augustine, Florida, where he went to recuperate, he wrote in his *Journals*: "He has seen but half the Universe who never has been shown the house of Pain. Pleasure and Peace are but indifferent teachers. . . ."[63] Thus it is wrong to assume, as many critics do, that Emerson was a kind of naïve optimist who excluded evil from his view of life. Rather, he accepted it, as did the mystics, realized its value in self-understanding, and reached beyond it and intellectualized it in his philosophy. "Therefore," Emerson wrote in "Uriel," "Evil will bless, and ice will burn"; and in "Experience," "Of course it needs the whole of society to give the symmetry we seek. The party-colored wheel must revolve very fast to appear white." That is to say, " 'evil' in the conventional sense is often not really Evil, but either a possible means to good, or a practical or potential good."[64]

Emerson's view is also reechoed by Whitman in "Chanting the Square Deific," where Satan is installed as a fourth member of the Trinity of Father, Son, and Holy Ghost. The intention is that the Father, or the principle of authority, may at times be tyrannical and unjust, thus needing the principle of rebellion (Satan) to right the possible errors. Satan is thus seen to serve a good purpose. Thomas Jefferson, earlier, had said the same thing in political terms.[65] There are similar views expressed in Job, and by Blake in his comments on Milton's *Paradise Lost*. Job, by being made to suffer at the instigation of Satan, attains as a result a deeper and profounder knowledge of God. Blake called Satan the hero of *Paradise Lost* because of his stubborn rebelliousness in the face of overwhelming power and because Adam and Eve gained an awareness of evil, and thus a deeper level of existence. And it is for similar reasons that Whitman calls himself the poet of "wickedness" as well as goodness.

Aside from the "values of evil" enumerated above, Emerson says the following about evil in the overall sense.

Good is positive. Evil is merely privative, not absolute: it is like cold, which is the privation of heat. All evil is so much death of non-entity. Benevolence is absolute and real.[66]

Thus evil is the denial of life or power. The greatest men are those who receive the most divine energy, or as Emerson would put it, those who are willing receptacles of the infusions of the Oversoul. Those who obstruct and fail of reception are the wicked ones, for evil is simply the privation of this prescience and power.[67]

Historical Christianity asserts that a man is punished or rewarded in his future life for his conduct in this life. Emerson early records his differences with the doctrine of the retribution of sins. In his *Journals* he wrote that somehow the universe was moral; it rose up against those who committed crimes and punished them in the here and now. "Suppose a tyrant arises and destroys the peace and good order of one community after another, and of nation after nation." That tyrant must cease because "Day and Night contend against him; the Elements which he wielded rebel and crush him: the clouds nurse their thunders to blast him; he is lifted upon rebellious spears between heaven and earth, unworthy and abhorred by both to perish."[68] For Emerson, then, punishment does not follow but accompanies crime. In the moral and physical spheres these is an equilibrium of opposite forces. The universe was so created that it contains within itself the means of balancing out any moral imperfection. Thus he expounds his famous Law of Compensation.

> Every spiritual law, I suppose, would be a contradiction to common sense. Thus I should begin with my old saws, that nothing can be given; every thing is sold; love completes love; hatred, hatred; action and reaction always are equal; no evil in society but has its check which coexists; the moral, the physical, the social world is a plenum, and any flood in one place produces equal ebb in another; nothing is free but the will of man, and that only to procure his own virtue; on every side but that one beats the air with his pompous action; that punishment not follows but accompanies crime.[69]

Throughout his writings Emerson always refers to the "moral sentiment," the "moral law," the "moral sense"; it was his abiding concern throughout his life. He had said quite early in his career that "Milton did not love moral perfection any more than he." His whole philosophy is an expression of his desire to elevate the soul of man; to improve character. Within man are contained the seeds of divinity; therefore the function of the teacher is "to acquaint man with himself." One does not become moral by suddenly following prescribed codes of conduct, divinely ordained or not. By morality, Emerson means "the direction of the will on universal ends." He is immoral whose actions are directed toward a private end. "He is moral—we say with Marcus Aurelius and with Kant—whose aim or motive may become a universal rule, binding on all intelligent beings."[70] If one so perceives the overarching Law of the Universe, and allows himself to merge with it, his actions then will be moral—they will be directed toward universal ends. For

> all things are moral. That soul which within us is a sentiment, outside of us is a law. We feel its inspiration; but

there in history we can see its fatal strength. "It is in the world, and the world was made by it." Justice is not postponed. A perfect equity adjusts its balance in all parts of life.... The dice of God are always loaded. The world looks like a multiplication table, or a mathematical equation, which turn it how you will, balances itself.... Every secret is told, every crime is punished, every virtue rewarded, every wrong redressed, in silence and certainty.[71]

A comparison of Emerson's Oversoul with the God of historical Christianity illustrates still another difference between natural religion and traditional faith. The traditional view of God is that of a personal Deity who is referred to in anthropomorphic terms. His relationship with man is that of the all-knowing, wise father who looks after the well-being of his children, and who metes out rewards and punishments. God has created the world out of a formless mass, and thus nature is not an embodiment of the Deity but His handiwork. God remains above the creation and makes his will known to man by injecting Himself in human affairs through supernatural occurrences, such as the burning bush, the pillar of fire, the incarnation of Jesus Christ, etc. The deists, for the most part, also conceived of God as a loving Father, and the Creator of a perfect universe. But they felt that once God created the world, he stood aloof from his creation and took little part in human history. In addition, they rejected supernaturalism and mystery—God did not act by interruption of natural law. He is not a "magician and wonder-worker," or a "potter" who molded man on his wheel. With the advent of the transcendental movement, particularly in the works of Emerson, the conception of God in natural religion takes on a different and more mystical cast. The Oversoul is not a personal god in the sense that it can be communed with, as man communes with God in the Old Testament via dialogue and covenants. Rather, the Oversoul is a vast impersonal spiritual substance which pervades the whole creation, and exists equally in the smallest clod and the most sublime human being. All of the creation is submerged in this sea, and there is no metaphysical separation of the inanimate, animate, and spiritual realms; there are no breaks or levels as in Christian theology:

the heart in thee is the heart of all; not a valve, not a wall, not an intersection is there anywhere in nature, but one blood rolls uninterruptedly in endless circulation through all men, as the water of the globe is all one sea, and truly seen its tide is one. Let man then learn the revelation of all nature and all thought to his heart; this namely; that the Highest dwells within him; that the sources of nature are in his own mind.[72]

Emerson was attacked by the Unitarians for not believing in a personal God. Norton claimed that God could not exist as other objects exist, a unity in a multiplicity of objects distinct from them all as they are distinct from each other, each knowable. To think of God in this manner was to bring him down to the level of the finite.[73] When a friend wrote to Emerson on the subject, he answered, "personality, too, and impersonality, might each be affirmed of the Absolute Being; and what may not be affirmed of it, in our own mind? And when we have heaped a mountain of speeches, we have still to begin again having nowise expressed the simple unalterable fact."[74] Again, in his *Journals,* Emerson comes to an unsettled answer.

What shall I answer to these friendly youths who ask of me an account of Theism, and think the views I have expressed on the impersonality of God desolating and ghastly? I say that I cannot find, when I explore my own consciousness, any truth in stating that God is a person, but the reverse. I feel that there is some profanation in saying He is personal. To represent Him as an individual is to shut Him out of my consciousness. He is then but a great man such as the crowd worships. Yet, yet, *Cor purgat oratio.*[75]

Emerson's view of the Deity was greatly influenced by his reading of both Eastern and Western mystics. He was an ardent reader of Plotinus, and reveals familiarity with Meister Eckhart and Jacob Boehm. His oriental studies increased in his later years, and it is to both these sources that one must go to understand better how Emerson thinks of God.

The mystics conceive of God as an ocean of light, or reservoir of spiritual power from which divine energy flows or emanates to the individual soul. The theory of emanation is common to most schools of mysticism. The world is conceived of as coming into existence not through God's operating upon matter as in traditional religion, but by a series of emanations from the central source—the World Soul. The universe, then, is an incarnation of God; his spirit is everywhere and pervades matter. We are so many sparks thrown off by the central emanator, and contain within us the God-substance. In mystical thought God is closer to man than in historical Christianity. "There is no screen or ceiling between our heads and the infinite heavens, so there is no bar or wall in the soul, where man the effect ceases, and God the cause begins."[76] All man has to do, then, is to allow himself through intuition to realize this closeness and thus experience oneness with all things. In the following passage, from "The Oversoul," Emerson illustrates this closeness of man and God. Notice the use of the same words in lower and upper case to explain the relationship. One senses the incompleteness of man without God, and conversely God without man.

> The soul gives itself, alone, original and pure, to the Lonely, Original and Pure, who, on that condition, gladly inhabits, leads and speaks through it. . . . I, the imperfect, adore my own Perfect.[77]

Mysticism steers clear of any fixed attributes in describing the nature of the Deity. God cannot be defined in any positive manner; he is known intuitively, and is always more than a finite being can conceive. Here are the thoughts of the German mystic Meister Eckhart:

> God is nameless, for no man can either say or understand aught about him. If I say God is good, it is not true; nay more; I am good, God is not good. I may even say, I am

better than God; for whatever is good, may become better: And if He cannot become better, he cannot become best. For these three things, good, better and best, are far from God, since He is above all. If I also say God is wise, it is true: I am wiser than He. If I also say God is a Being, it is not true: He is transcendent Being and superessential nothingness.[78]

The Hindu mystics likewise describe the soul in negative terms, and all are insufficient to encompass its transcendental vastness. The moment one reduces the absolute to an object of worship, it becomes something less than the absolute; the unknowable is given form, the universal is made personal, the omnipresent is posited in a fixed location. Personality would imply a distinction of the self and the not-self, and hence is inapplicable to the All which embraces everything. The Oversoul of Emerson and the Brahma of the Hindus have much in common. Brahma is

without and within all beings. He is unmoving, as also moving. He is too subtle to be known. He is far away and yet He is near.

He is undivided (indivisible) and yet He seems to be divided among beings. He is to be known as supporting creatures, destroying them and creating them afresh.

He is the Light of lights, said to be beyond darkness. Knowledge, the object of knowledge, and the goal of knowledge—He is seated in the hearts of all. . . .

He who sees the Lord abiding equally in all beings, never perishing when they perish, he, verily, sees.

For, as he sees the Lord present equally everywhere, he does not injure his true Self by the self and then he attains to the supreme goal. . . .

When he sees that the manifold states of beings are centered in the One and from just that it spreads out, then he attains Brahma.[79]

Aside from direct influence of the Bhagavad-Gita on Emerson's poem "Brahma," the *Essays* also afford striking parallels to the Indian Scriptures. In "The Oversoul," Emerson writes:

> We live in succession, in division, in parts, in particles. Meantime within man is the soul of the whole; the wise silence; the universal beauty, to which every part and particle is equally related; the eternal One. And this deep power in which we exist and whose beatitude is all accessible to us, is not only self-sufficing and perfect in every hour, but the act of seeing and the thing seen, the seer and the spectacle, the subject and the object, are one.[80]

Specifically, the last excerpt from the Bhagavad-Gita, quoted above is paralleled by the following: "In ascending to this primary and aboriginal sentiment [Divine Mind] we have come from our remote station on the circumference instantaneously to the center of the world, where, as in the closet of God, we see causes, and anticipate the universe, which is but a slow effect."[81]

Emerson's Oversoul and the Hindu Brahma seem to be pantheistic deities. But upon closer examination we find that this is not necessarily true. Most types of pantheism assert that God is everywhere and that nature is the body of God. For Emerson and the Hindu mystics the Deity is still greater than the world which subsists in it. Emerson, in the following quotation, explains the transcendent quality of the Oversoul.

> The world proceeds from the same spirit as the body of man. It is a remoter and inferior incarnation of God, a projection of God in the unconscious. But it differs from the body in one important respect. It is not, like that, now subjected to the human will. Its serene order is inviolable by us. It is, therefore, to us, the present expositer of the divine mind.[82]

And:

> The soul is superior to its knowledge, wiser than any of its works.[83]

Emerson's conception of the Oversoul differs, however, in one important way from oriental mysticism. The latter is a static mysticism, Emerson's is dynamic. For the goal of the Hindu is to achieve eternal rest in Brahma. He views the world as a veil or as "maya," and by self-discipline and ascetic practices endeavors to pierce the veil to the vision of Oneness. Once attaching this state, the religious votary has not further use for the world or society—indeed, the world is an illusion. Emerson at times almost denies the existence of matter as in the section, "Idealism" in *Nature*, but he does not go so far as the Indian sages in this respect; he preached a balance between activity and contemplation. He felt that the cosmic process was developing to the perfection of its central source—the Oversoul, and man, by his true actions and the direction of his will, assists in this development. Yet this incessant movement and development in which all things partake could never have any meaning to us "but by contrast to some principle of fixture or stability in the soul."

Whilst the eternal generation of circles proceeds, the eternal generator abides.[84]

And this central life is somewhat superior to creation, superior to knowledge and thought, and within it contains all the evolving circles. "Forever it labors to create a life and thought as large and excellent as itself." Therefore it is wrong to rest on established beliefs or ideas, because everything is moving forward. Each advance is the means to another, and so on *ad infinitum*. He exhorts us not to set the least value on what he does, or the least discredit on what he does not do, if he pretends to settle anything as true or false.

I unsettle all things. No facts to me are sacred; none profane; I simply experiment, an endless seeker with no past at my back.[85]

For Emerson history is of little value, tradition an impediment; the reasoning process is inadequate to tap the knowledge of the soul. We are receptacles of the Divine Spirit, and must constantly keep ourselves open to its calling. The inherent dynamic quality of Emerson's thought is expressed in the following quotation, which illustrates his abiding concern that established beliefs are contrary to the operation of the universe and human destiny:

> In nature every moment is new; the past is always swallowed and forgotten; the coming only is sacred. Nothing is secure but life, transition, the energizing spirit. No love can be bound by oath or covenant to secure it against a higher love. No truth so sublime but it may be trivial to-morrow in the light of new thoughts. People wish to be settled; only so far as they are unsettled is there any hope for them.[86]

Emerson's purpose was to make man aware that he possessed within himself the deepest spiritual truths. Hence, Emerson often said that it was the function of the teacher to acquaint man with his own divinity. In so doing, Emerson became his age's strongest critic. Historical Christianity had become timid and ineffectual, and Emerson and the transcendentalists saw the need to advocate a more dynamic union of man, God and nature—one that would revitalize man's spiritual energy. Emerson is broader and more profound in his thinking than Theodore Parker. His ideas are subtle and complex, an amalgam of German transcendentalism and neoplatonic and oriental mysticism. Emerson, however, was not simply eclectic; all his borrowings from the thoughts of others are suffused with a plastic unifying vision. He is unique; his thought is the most original of the figures in natural religion in American literature. Ethan Allen, Paine, Freneau and Jefferson, the eighteenth-century deists, were not overly original in their writings, but in the main borrowed from the English deists. In their hatred of priestcraft and supernaturalism the deists were, in a large part, motivated by the current revolutionary zeal. They reflected the typical eighteenth-century inclination of not trusting intuition or the poetic imagination, and would have been impatient with the mystical element within transcendentalism. Their god was, in general, a distant, rationalistic, mechanistic overseer of man and the creation, in comparison with the intimate, all-pervading, all-embracing Oversoul. In addition, although the deists spoke of the "common notions" in all religion, and proclaimed them to be the basis of natural religion, they nowhere asserted this with the prophetic ardor of Parker and Emerson. The "new teacher" that Emerson refers to at the close of the "Divinity School Address" will unite the moral teachings of the Old and New Testaments with the laws of science. The excerpt can be taken as a summation of Emerson's lifelong vision and hope:

> I look for the hour when that supreme Beauty which ravished the souls of those Eastern men, and chiefly those Hebrews, and through their lips spoke oracles to all time, shall speak in the West also. The Hebrew and Greek Scriptures contain immortal sentences, that have been bread of life to millions. But they have no epical integrity; are fragmentary; are not shown in their order to the intellect. I look for the new Teacher that shall follow so far those shining laws that he shall see them come full circle; shall see their rounding complete grace; shall see the world to be the mirror of the soul; shall see the identity of the law of gravitation with purity of heart; and shall show that the Ought, that Duty, is one thing with Science, with Beauty, and with Joy.[87]

Later Emerson was to think that with the publication of *Leaves of Grass*, Whitman was the new teacher or new poet who would embody the truth he sought to make known; but this admiration of Whitman was tempered by the latter's inclusion of sensuality in his poem.

It was on Whitman, indeed, that the mantle of natural religion was placed, Emerson's qualification notwithstanding. Whitman's ideas are very similar to the Concord Seer's, although he expresses them in the raw metaphors of the American environment. Temperamentally they were at odds with each other. The philosopher of the Oversoul dwelt primarily in the realm of intellect; he started from the abstract and worked down to the particular. Whitman, on the other hand, started from the concrete and specific and worked up to the general and the abstract. He gave natural religion roots in the physical and sensual, and exhalted democracy into a spiritual ideal.

CHAPTER SEVEN

Walt Whitman

In the writings of Walt Whitman natural religion reaches its culmination in American literature. Whitman's religion of the common man embraces the ideals of the deists who rejected the authority of church and priest and the pantheism of the transcendentalists. But Whitman did more than synthesize their thought; he added much that was original. Although he owed a debt to his precursors, especially Emerson, he carried on the tradition of independent religious thought in America to its highest point of development in the nineteenth century.

Whitman's religion of the "divine average" contains the ideas of equality and individual freedom expressed in the Declaration of Independence and the Constitution. His concept of a "spiritual democracy" is permeated with the belief that religion must not only concern the individual, but is and must be the basis of the state. His thought, though holding much in common with transcendentalism, is more socially oriented. In fact, it was for this lack of sufficient social and human concern that Whitman criticized Emerson.[1] The Yankee thinker was superb in developing his theory of the Oversoul. He expounded with Olympian serenity the beauty of the spiritual laws, but seldom descended into the arena of men and events. Thus, for Whitman, his philosophy was too limited and one-sided. Whitman loved his fellow man, indeed all of the creation; and it was this underlying sympathy for life itself that was the basis of all his poetry.

Yet both these writers reveal strong similarities in their basic thought despite their differences in emphasis and temperament. They were thinkers whose ideas ranged beyond the local and the traditional; they both distrusted logic and definition and stressed intuition, direct communion with the soul; they both believed in a constant process of evolutionary development in man, society, and religion. Consequently, they were impatient with those who venerated a dead past and a frigid, impotent present. They looked to the future for the realization of their respective ideals. Emerson was always referring to the "new teacher" who would carry out the synthesis he sought between moral and physical laws; Whitman looked to the coming of the divine "literatus" who would unite in his poems America's material and spiritual potentials. In a word, both men were prophetic and visionary; Whitman to a greater degree. They were seers and asserters who expounded the divinity of man and held a firm optimistic faith in the future of democracy. Pessimism, morbidity, dwelling upon the darker motives in men's minds were foreign to them. Whitman was aware of the crudity, vulgarity and corruption of his times, and though he recorded his dismay with his current America, he felt, nevertheless, that the future would bring out the best. Emerson writing in an earlier, more golden era seemed totally unaware of the ambiguity of human nature and the dangers of the growing materialism. William James classified this type of religious optimism as the "Religion of Healthy-Mindedness." James cited Spinoza, Berkeleian Idealism, and the Christian Science Mind Cure movement along with Emerson and Whitman as representative of healthy-minded religion. James pointed out that these philosophies have the tendency to look at all things "and see that they are good. . . . Systematic healthy-mindedness conceiving good as the essential and universal aspect of being, deliberately excludes evil from its field of vision."[2] Another belief of these philosophies is that man is already one with the Divine "without any miracle of grace, or abrupt creation of the inner man." James continues:

> The great central fact of the universe is that spirit of infinite life and power that is back of all, that manifests itself in and through all. This spirit of infinite life and power that is back of all is what I call God. I care not what term you may use, be it Kindly Light, Providence, the Over-Soul, Omnipotence, or whatever term may be most convenient, so long as we are agreed in regard to the great central fact itself. God then fills the universe alone, so that all is from Him and in Him, and there is nothing that is outside. He is the life of our life, our very life itself. We are partakers of the life of God; and though we differ from Him in that we are individualized spirits, while He is the Infinite Spirit, including us, as well as all else beside, yet in essence the life of God and the life of man are identically the same, and so are one. They differ not in essence or quality; they differ in degree.[3]

This religious category of James's explains Whitman's acceptance of the world and life as it is ("There will never be any more perfection than there is now")[4]. This is because the world and man are permeated with the spirit of God; or, in Emerson's terms we are "part and parcel" of the central Perfection—the Oversoul.

In Whitman's natural religion there is much less criticism leveled against historical Christianity than we found among the deists and transcendentalists. One of the reasons for this lack of vigorous criticism of institutional religion is that Whitman came from a Quaker background, unlike Emerson and Parker whose thought evolved amid New England Calvinism and Unitarianism about which there was a history of sharp debate and interpretation of religious doctrines as has been shown, and in which Emerson and Parker were naturally emersed. Hence their expression of natural religion reveals more militancy toward historical Christianity. In contrast to the intense theological debates between Calvinists, Unitarians, and transcendentalists, "the Quaker's passivity had allowed the growth of an undisturbed depth of emotion. . . . The sympathetic kinship that Emerson felt in his liberated maturity with Quakerism had belonged with Whitman as his birthright."[5] However, it would be wrong to assume that Whitman made no unfavorable references to institutional religion; scattered throughout his poetry and prose there are a good number of such criticisms which will be discussed presently. One example will suffice here: "religion must extricate itself entirely from the churches. . . ."[6]

Although the aim of this chapter is not to make an exhaustive comparison of Emerson's and Whitman's thought, it is necessary that some comparison be drawn so that we can see how Whitman's ideas fit into the trend of natural religion and in what ways he added to and enriched that movement. Whitman in his passionate concern for originality tried to play down the influence that Emerson and others may have had on his thinking. This, however, was true during the period he was striving for recognition and acclaim as the great American poet. Early he confessed that he "was simmering, simmering; Emerson brought me to a boil."[7] But later on, probably when the relationship between the two men had cooled because of Emerson's second thoughts about the inclusion of sexuality ("Children of Adam" and "Calamus") in *Leaves of Grass,* Whitman claimed that Emerson had little influence upon him. Responding to a letter from a friend who had asked him if he had read Emerson before writing *Leaves of Grass,* he denied having done so, saying that he finds everything in the common and the concrete, the flesh and the passions. "I radiate . . . outwards," he said; "this is the antipodes of Emerson."[7a]

Thus, unlike Emerson who at times doubted the existence of the external world, Whitman accepted and glorified it. For Emerson the world was *symbolic* of the Spirit or Oversoul, it was "the present *expositor* of the divine mind."[8] Nature was an emblem for for the mind of man to read and understand, and by so doing reach God. Whitman is no philosophic idealist; for him matter is the equal of spirit.

> I accept Reality and dare not question it,
> Materialism first and last imbuing.[9]

Emerson reacted strongly against the Unitarian view of the finiteness and imperfection of man and advocated his divinity. Nevertheless, he qualified his position, lapsing back at times into the old mind-body dualism; "human life and its persons are poor empirical pretensions."

> I cannot often enough say that a man is only a relative and representative nature. Each is a hint of the truth, but far enough from being the truth which yet he quite newly and inevitably suggests to us.[10]

Whitman's faith never wavers on this point. Both the body and the spirit within man are equally divine.

> I believe in the flesh, and the appetites,
> Seeing, hearing, feeling are miracles, and each
>   part and tag of me is a miracle.
>
> Divine am I inside and out, and I make holy
>   whatever I touch or am touch'd from,
> The scent of these arm-pits aroma finer than prayer,
>
> This head more than churches, bibles and all the creeds.[11]

Both men, however were united in their distrust of logic. Truth was not to be pursued by argument and proposition. Both maintained that intuition was the only way to attain an understanding of reality. Emerson said that we are receptacles of the divine spirit which in sublime moments pours knowledge into us. "Logic," he maintained, "is the procession or proportionate unfolding of the intuition. . . ."

> Our thinking is a pious reception, . . . We do not determine what we think. We only open our senses, clear away as we can all obstruction from the fact and suffer the intellect to see.[12]

Whitman inveighs continually against all formulas and logical systems of thought. The test of wisdom is not in the "schools." "Wisdom is of the soul, is not susceptible of proof, is its own

proof."[13] Like Emerson, Whitman says the highest truth infil-
trates the soul in those deepest moments of spiritual insight:

> Here is the efflux of the soul,
> The efflux of the soul comes from within through
>   embowered gates, ever provoking questions.[14]

Another point on which Emerson and Whitman agree is the
sense of identity between man and nature. Indeed, romanticism
in general advocates this central conviction. In the previous
chapter we discussed Emerson's version of this relationship:
man must so align his vision with the axis of things that the
Universal Being will fill him and all things will be seen to be
perfect and transparent. Whitman's version is somewhat different. Emerson's unifying agency, we note, is vision, or an act
of the mind. He developed an intricate theory of correspondence by which the mind read the symbols of spirit all about him
in the natural world. Whitman, less the philosopher than the
poet, assumes identity from the first, and needs no doctrine
of correspondence. Although if one looked carefully enough
in his poems one could probably find something like Emerson's
idea of correspondence. "I see something of God each hour of
the twenty-four, and each moment then,/In the faces of men
and women I see God, and in my own face in the glass,/I find
letters from God dropt in the street, and everyone is signed by
God's name . . ."[15] But this is a poetic technique by which
Whitman expresses the equation of the natural world with God,
and not a consistently carried out philosophical idea.

A brief examination of the term "pantheism" may help to shed
more light on this distinction. Gay Wilson Allen in discussing
pantheism in connection with Whitman's thought points out the
complexity and various meanings of the term. For instance, the
dictionary definition indicates two contradictory viewpoints:
"The doctrine that the universe, taken or conceived as a whole,
is God; the doctrine that there is no God but the combined
forces and laws which are manifested in the existing universe."
The first suggests a spiritual pantheism, the second a material-

istic pantheism—which some scholars deny being pantheism at all. The latter version is often associated with atheism, and has been attacked by theologians for its denying personality to the deity.[16]

In most versions, however, pantheism is neither atheistic or agnostic, but is a mystical belief in the oneness of mind, matter and God. The creation has emanated from God, who does not stand apart from the creation, but is conceived of as being "immanent," or existing within it. Dr. Allen discusses several types of pantheism, the systems of Giordano Bruno, Spinoza, Leibnitz. Although Plotinus and Neoplatonism may be considered the ancient source of Western pantheism, "Spinoza is usually regarded as the father of modern pantheism."[17] His ideas influenced and formed the background of German Idealism, which is one of the sources for Emerson's and Whitman's unique forms of pantheism. Spinoza taught

> that proof of God is the existence of nature, and that the created and the creator are one; hence that it is not necessary to go outside the realm of nature to find God. Since God is indivisible, nature is interlocked by an all-pervading unity. If evil exists at all, it must exist in nature, and nature being indivisible, there is no evil; or what we call evil is only what displeases us. When the mind by intuitive insight catches a glimpse of God in nature, it perceives the immortal, which is to say, outside Time and Space (which have no more reality than evil). Thus immortality may be achieved here and now by the mind's identifying itself with God-in-nature.[18]

For Leibnitz the "monads," the ultimate reality, are indestructible; therefore there is really no birth nor death and the soul continues on to other stages of existence. In his theory of the Ego, Fichte maintains that "nature is physical in appearances but spiritual in reality and that thought—Idea—is the only Reality." Central to Schelling's philosophy is the belief that "the outer world is symbolic of the real or ideal (thought) world;

in nature we see the *identity* of the ideal." Whitman summarized this doctrine as follows:

> *the essential identity of the subjective and objective worlds,* or ... what exists as mentality, intelligence, consciousness in man, exists in equal strength and absoluteness in concrete forms, shows [i.e. appearances] and practical laws in material nature.[19]

In conclusion Dr. Allen says, "Some pantheists tend to deny reality of any kind to the physical world, regarding it as illusory and evanescent, while others regard it as Divine Reality itself."[20] Whitman, then, falls into that general category of pantheism which regards the world virtually as the Divine Reality, while Emerson is closer to the first type, which doubts the reality of the visible world. However, one cannot maintain this unequivocally in Emerson's case, for the advocate of the Oversoul straddles the fence on this point. Perhaps a better term for Emerson's position is "panentheism" as discussed in the previous chapter.[21] Panentheism is the belief that the world is not a complete manifestation of the Absolute, or in the way in which Emerson would phrase it, the world "is a remote and inferior incarnation of God, a projection of God in the unconscious."[22]

Natural religion in Whitman then gains a new dimension and direction. The physical world is seen not as a revelation or symbol of the Divine, but the Divine itself. The body is the equal of the soul, objects in nature all merge with the identifying self in a mystical oneness. Everything is equal and of one piece. Whitman identifies himself with all humanity, with the animate and inanimate world: the earth, the stars, dust, grains of sand, insects, and so on.

Emerson said that man only applied half his force to nature. By not perceiving the world by intuition, it seemed broken and lacking in unity. The remedy he prescribed was that man must be simultaneously a naturalist and a spiritualist. However, he declared, "in actual life the marriage is not celebrated."[23] What required a special act of perception for Emerson, to Whitman was an accepted reality. By mystical intuition he experienced the *reality* of God and His creation:

> And I know that the hand of God is the promise
> of my own,
> And I know that the spirit of God is the brother
> of my own,
> And that all the men ever born are also my brothers,
> and the women my sisters and lovers,
> And that a kelson of the creation is love,
> And limitless are leaves stiff or drooping in
> the fields,
> And brown ants in the little wells beneath them,
> And mossy scabs of the worm fence, heap'd stones,
> elder, mullein and poke-weed.[24]

Whitman absorbs all things within him, thus enlarging the self so that it fills and merges with the whole universe. This is both mystical and pantheistic. "I take part, I see and hear the whole." In his catalogues of events, people, places that he is constantly unrolling before us, he is always present, always a part, experiencing and identifying himself with what he describes. "I am the man, I suffer'd, I was there."[25]

Thus it can be seen that Emerson's Oversoul was more nearly the Hindu Brahma than Whitman's vital, fleshly "I" through which the poet identifies himself with all of the creation. Emerson always exhalted the infinitude of the private man. Whitman contains this idea, but would not rest content there; the individual is unique and divine, true, but by himself he is only partially complete. Only when he merges or identifies himself through sympathy and love with all men does he attain the mystic union with the soul, with God. Whitman's thought stresses equally the vertical relationship of the individual with God and the horizontal relationship of the individual with his fellow man.

> Underneath all, individuals,
> I swear nothing is good to me now that ignores individuals,
> The American compact is altogether with individuals, ...
> The whole theory of the universe is directed unerringly to
> one single individual—namely to You

And a few lines further on he declares:

> Underneath all is the Expression of love for men and
>   women.[26]

This idea of the sacredness of the individual in common and
equal bond with other individuals is an inherent part of Whitman's thought. Hence the declaration, "One's-self I sing, a
simple separate person,/Yet utter the word Democratic, the
word En-Masse."[27]

The dialectic sometimes uses the terms the "Me" and the
"Not-Me," sometimes it consists of three, the soul, other souls,
nature. And always the unifying force is identity, the means
of identity, sympathy, or love. Whitman had written in one of the
many anonymous reviews of his own book of poems:

> The most profound theme that can occupy the mind of
> man ... is doubtless involved in the query: What is the
> fusing explanation and tie—what is the relation between
> the (radical, democratic) Me, the human identity of under-
> standing, emotions, spirit, & etc., on the one side, ... with
> the (conservative) Not-Me, the whole of the material
> universe and laws, with what is behind them in time and
> space, on the other side?[28]

And so the very theme of "Song of Myself" answers the question.
It is a song of identification; "I do not ask the wounded person
how he feels,/I myself become the wounded person,/I am the
hounded slave, I wince at the bite of the dogs," or again, "Not
a youngster is taken for larceny but I go up too, and am tried
and sentenced." There are countless such examples in Whitman's
other poems as well, in which he projects himself into other
identities. Nor is there a loss of his own identity in the process.
He both fully realizes the unique identity of his separate
self and the identities of that self with other selves.

> I go from bedside to bedside, I sleep close with
>   the other sleepers each in turn,
> I dream in my dream all the dreams of the other
>   dreamers,
> And I become the other dreamers. . . .

I am the actor, the actress, the voter, the
    politician,
The emigrant and the exile, the criminal that
    stood in the box,
He who has been famous and he who shall be
    famous after today,
The stammerer, the well-formed person, the
    waster or feeble person.[29]

Whitman added another concept to the development of natural
religion. It is a concept as old as human thought itself, reaching far back into the dawn of primitive religions—the idea of
transmigration of souls. Heretofore neither deism nor transcendentalism had worked this idea into natural religion in any
consistent degree. The after-life of the soul was a natural
outcome and inherent part of Whitman's pantheism. In "To
Think of Time," he says that if one thinks of death as an ultimate finality one is making a profound error, because by so
doing one denies "soul" for every particle of the universe.

I swear I think that every thing without exception
    has an eternal soul!
The trees have, rooted in the ground! the weeds of
    the sea have! the animals!
I swear I think there is nothing but immortality!
That the exquisite scheme is for it, and the nebulous
    float is for it—and identity is for it—and life
    and materials are for it.[30]

In Whitman's pantheism the material world has the attributes of
the spiritual (i.e., it transcends time and space, it is thought
of as being eternal; though its forms change nothing is lost).
The world is conceived of as constantly developing and evolving.
As each object comes into the world, it is individualized
momentarily; that is, it receives identity through form or body
"and represents some portion of the soul-stuff which pervades
the universe."[31] But it continues on its journey returning to
the great germinating world soul, and reappearing in nature
in other forms in an endless cycle. The term "float," for instance,
Whitman probably got from the cosmic evolutionary theory

of Leibnitz and others. "This then is life, here is what has come
to the surface after so many throes and convulsions,..."[32]

> There is no stoppage and never can be stoppage,
> If I, you, and the worlds, and all beneath or upon
>   their surfaces, were this moment reduced back
>   to a pallid float, it would not avail in the
>   long run,
> We should surely bring up again where we now stand,
> And surely go as much farther, and then farther
>   and farther.[33]

Like most pantheists, Whitman does not fear death, but views
it as part of the cosmic plan. Souls are indestructible, and
unceasingly circulate from body to body and place to place,
each has its appointed abode, always promulgating some divine
scheme.

> I think it is not for life I am chanting here...
> I think it must be for death....[34]

Death and life are elements in the cosmic cycle and evolution,
and to fear death as a cessation of being is false. It is obvious that Whitman's attitude toward death is different from
the way in which the Christian views it. For the latter, it
can be a realm of everlasting peace in heaven, or a place of
everlasting punishment in the flames of hell. In either condition
the soul does not return to a state of existence in nature. In
Whitman's cosmic pantheism there are endless deaths and births.

> I have sung...the song of life and Birth—and
>   shown that there are many births.[35]

In fact, he even proclaims it may be "luckier" to die than to
be born.[36] I believe he overstates his point here, to shock the
reader out of the traditional way of thinking about the subject,
and to make clearer that one is no better or worse than the
other.

> Death or life I am then indifferent, my soul
>   declines to prefer.[37]

It has been pointed out by many critics that Whitman's "I" is generic and cosmic rather than personal, but it can be also mentioned that there is almost an infinite range of his "I" as a representative migrating "soul."

> I exist as I am, that is enough,
> If no other in the world be aware I sit content,
> And if each and all be aware I sit content.
>
> One world is aware and by far the largest to me,
>   and that is myself,
> And whether I come to my own to-day or in ten-
>   thousand or ten million years,
>
> I can cheerfully take it now, or with equal cheer-
>   fulness I can wait.
>
> My foothold is tenon'd and mortised in granite,
> I laugh at what you call dissolution
> And I know the amplitude of time....
>
> And as to you Life, I reckon you are the leavings
>   of many deaths,
> (No doubt I have died myself ten thousand times before)
> I hear you whispering there O stars of heaven,
> O suns—O grass of graves—O perpetual transfers
>   and promotions....[38]

Whitman's pantheism is set off from that of the Bhagavad-Gita in that he does not depict the soul as retrogressing into a lower state of existence. For the Hindu believer born to the lower castes is doomed to an endless cycle of rebirths in lower animal and inanimate forms; his goal is to try to escape rebirth. By practicing yoga and mind control he can avoid the ceaseless cycle and reach a state of Oneness or Brahma. This state once achieved, the soul is free from transmigration and rests serene and inviolate. But not so for Whitman. Since he views each particle of the universe as equally divine, there are no levels of lower or higher existence. The creation is "no less than a complete and uncompromising cosmic democracy!"[39] In addition the soul (the "I" in Whitman's poems) "tramps a perpetual journey." Thus in "Song of Myself," he writes:

I believe a leaf of grass is no less than the
    journey-work of the stars,
And the pismire is equally perfect, and a grain
    of sand, and the egg of the wren,
And the tree-toad is a chef-d'oeuvre for the highest,
And the running blackberry would adorn the parlors
    of heaven. . . .

I find I incorporate gneiss, coal, long-threaded moss,
    esculent roots
And am stucco'd with quadrupeds and birds all over,
And have distanced what is behind me and for good
    reasons,
And call anything back again when I desire it.[40]

When he says that he can "call any thing back again" when he desires it, this is not to be taken in a literal sense. Whitman is poetically identifying himself with the World Soul which operates in this way. His sympathy with the animals, however, is more than poetic identification. He is the journeying soul forever through time and incorporating within himself all creatures.

I wonder where they get those tokens,
Did I pass that way huge times ago and negligently
    drop them?
Myself moving forward then and now and forever,
Gathering and showing more always and with velocity,
Infinite and omnigenous, . . .

A gigantic beauty of a stallion, fresh and responsive
    to my caresses, . . .
His well-built limbs tremble with pleasure as we race
    around and return.
I but use you a minute, then resign you, stallion,
Why do I need your paces when I myself outgallop them?
Even as I stand or sit passing faster than you.[41]

It is within the scope of this vision that the poet feels himself to be "an acme of things accomplished" and "an encloser of things to be."[42] And it is also in this sense that he glorifies his own body and his forebears:

> Before I was born out of my mother generations
> guided me,
> My embryo has never been torpid, nothing could
> over-lay it.[43]

His heredity goes back to the origin of the creation. His soul was present at and saw the "huge first Nothing,"

> I know I was even there,
> I waited unseen and always, and slept through the
> lethargic mist,
>
> And took my time, and took no hurt from the fetid
> carbon. . . .
> All forces have been steadily employed to complete
> and delight me,
> Now on this spot I stand with my robust soul.[44]

Now it can be seen that when Whitman says "nothing, not even God is greater to one than oneself is," he is not deifying his ego, but the Self within, the cosmic Soul. The same can be said for Emerson on this point; "Self Reliance" does not refer to the self, in the ordinary sense, but to God, or the Oversoul.

Whitman's doctrine of the evolution of the soul accounts for his worship of sex, "for it is by means of sex that the soul receives its identity and perpetually fulfills the cosmic plan."[45]

> Ages and ages returning at intervals,
> Undestroy'd, wandering immortal,
> Lusty, phallic, with the potent original loins, . . .[46]

Almost the whole of "Children of Adam" exemplifies this idea, and its basis is philosophical rather than personal. It is true, of course, that Whitman exploited this idea as a means of indicating his objections to asceticism and prudery, but he considered asceticism to be philosophically at odds with his own ideas. And again, it is probably true that his own temperament may have re-enforced the conviction and caused it to take such a strong hold on him. But this is probably true of every man's ideas. It is this glorification of the body and sexuality which sets Whitman's thought apart not only from historical Christianity, but from his forerunners in natural religion, the deists and transcendentalists. One could imagine the Unitarians as well as the young New England transcendentalists shuddering at almost any passage of *Children of Adam* which eulogizes in minute detail the anatomy of male and female. What can be further from St. Paul than the following:

> And if the body does not do fully as much as the soul?
> And if the body were not the soul, what is the soul? . . .
>
> Have you seen the fool that corrupted his own live body?
>   or the fool that corrupted her own live body?
> For they do not conceal themselves, and cannot conceal
>   themselves.[47]

Sex, he asserts, is natural and wholesome, guilt and shame is evil.

> The consequent meanness of me should I skulk or find
>   myself indecent, while birds and animals never once
>   skulk or find themselves indecent, . . .[48]

For, through the act of procreation new souls will come into the world and further the plan of cosmic evolution.

> The oath of procreation I have sworn, my Adamic and
>   fresh daughters, . . .
> I shall demand perfect men and women out of my love
>   spendings,
> I shall expect them to interpenetrate with others, as I
>   and you interpenetrate now, . . .
> I shall look for loving crops from the birth, life, death,
>   immortality, I plant so lovingly now.[49]

Whitman follows the deists and transcendentalists in his conception of a moral universe and his belief in the perfectibility of man. His ideas on morality are related to his cosmic pantheism. Although Whitman seldom speaks of "morality" *per se,* we can gather what his thoughts are on the subject indirectly by examining his general philosophy. One cannot expect to find logical consistency in Whitman; he himself tells us that he "contains contradictions." However, there is a polarity in his thought in regard to the ideal picture of man he presents so optimistically, and his awareness of the vulgarity and corruption in society. Thus, he can say, at one point, that "there will never be any more perfection than there is now,"[50] and seemingly contradict this in the poem, "As I Look Out," by telling us of the imperfections he sees all about him:

> I sit and look out upon all the sorrows of the world,
>   and upon all oppression and shame,
> I hear secret convulsive sobs from young men at anguish
>   with themselves, remorseful after deeds done,
> I see in low life the mother misused by her children,
>   dying, neglected, gaunt, desperate,
> I see the wife misused by her husband, I see the treacherous
>   seducer of young women, ...
> I see the workings of battle, pestilence, tyranny, I see
>   martyrs and prisoners, ...
> I observe the slights and degradations cast by arrogant
>   persons upon laborers, the poor, and upon negroes, and
>   the like;
> All these—all the meanness and agony without end I sitting
>   look out upon,
> See, hear, and am silent.[51]

The key to the apparent difficulty lies in the last line: "See, hear, and am silent." Whitman felt that moral imperfection was only a stage in the evolution of man and nature. Ultimate perfection he envisioned in the future; that is why he can remain silent knowing that what he sees will gradually wither away in the process of cosmic meliorization.

The same idea is presented in terms of physical deformities. Early in his notebook, he records that "a twisted skull, and blood watery or rotten by ancestry or gluttony, or rum, or bad disorders,—they are the darkness toward which the plant will not grow, although its seed lies waiting for ages."[52] And in his poetry the idea appears quite explicitly in "The Sleepers."

> The Soul is always beautiful,
> The universe is duly in order, everything is in its place,

What has arrived is in its place, and what waits shall be
in its place,
The twisted skull waits, the watery or rotten blood waits,
The child of the glutton or veneralee waits long, and the
child of the drunkard waits long, and the drunkard
himself waits long,
The sleepers that lived and died wait, the far advanced
are to go on in their turns, and the far behind are to
come on in their turns,
The diverse shall be no less diverse, but they shall flow
and unite—they unite now.[53]

In "Faces" the doctrine is once again presented:

Do you suppose I could be content with all (i.e., faces,
appearances) if I thought them their own finale?
. . . .
Of the word I have spoken I except not one—red, white,
black, are all deific,
In each house is the ovum, it comes forth after a thousand
years.
Spots or cracks at the windows do not disturb me,
Tall and sufficient stand behind and make signs to me,
I read the promise and patiently wait.[54]

This potential perfection in man and all things modifies to
a degree Whitman's glorification of the spirit incarnate in the
flesh. All beings and all life are in an incomplete state at
any given moment in their earthly "identities," but in the course
of cosmic evolution approach perfection.[55]
It can be understood, then, why Whitman could call himself
the poet of wickedness as well as goodness. His pantheism is
all-embracing, and evil is as much a part of the cosmic scheme
as virtue. Thus he writes:

I am not the poet of goodness only, I do not decline to
be the poet of wickedness also.

What blurt is this about virtue and vice?
Evil propels me and reform of evil propels me, I stand
indifferent
My gait is no fault-finders or rejectors gait; . . .[56]

Evil is as much a problem for pantheism as it is for institutional religion. For, if God pervades everything, as pantheism teaches, how can anything in the world be evil? In Christianity the problem is not resolved any easier, for if God is good, how can any part of His creation be bad? Christian theology attempts to answer the question by saying that God and man's great opponent in the cosmic drama is Satan; he is responsible for the evil in the world. This, however, is not a satisfactory solution, and admits the existence of not one God, but two, a greater and a lesser. The existence of evil in the world has been a stumbling block to theologians throughout the centuries, and it is the point seized upon by skeptics and critics of traditional faiths. The Hindu mystic, as discussed in the previous chapter, solves the problem by regarding evil as illusion; the mind is made to rise above the deception to a vision of Oneness. Emerson's solution is something like the Hindu approach. The deists regard evil as really good misunderstood. But man, being a finite creature, cannot see the overall plan.

Whitman's answer is not as clear cut as any of these, but he does give one which fits into his own pantheistic concepts. As has been shown, since he glorifies each part and parcel of the universe, he cannot omit the abnormal or the morally degenerate. In the following example he almost denies the existence of evil, but then qualifies it.

Omnes! omnes! let others ignore what they may,
I make the poem of evil also, I commemorate that part also,
I am myself just as much evil as good, and my nation is—
    and I say there is in fact no evil,
(Or if there is I say it is just as important to you, to the land or to me, as any thing else.)[57]

In the following passage he identifies himself with the most morally corrupt things:

I am he who knew what it was to be evil,
I too knitted the old knot of contrariety,
Blabb'd, blushed, resented, lied, stole, grudged,

Had guile, anger, lust, hot wishes I dared not speak,
Was wayward, vain, greedy, shallow, sly, cowardly,
    malignant,
The wolf, the snake, the hog, not wanting in me, . . .[58]

It is this flaunting of his worst characteristics and his com-
radely greeting of prostitutes and low characters, that caused
many critics to claim "that Whitman denied the existence of evil,
or at least refused to make moral distinctions."[59] But Whitman
does this for a reason; (Omnes! omnes!) he is the poet of *all*,
all things inanimate and animate, every object and particle of
the universe is equally perfect and necessary, and therefore good.
"In order to shock his readers into an awareness of the full
implication of this doctrine, he mentions the unmentionable,
dwells on the ugly, the crude, the taboo, not because they are
more important than the beautiful or the socially amenable, but
to force their inclusion in the whole of life, nature and the
cosmic scheme."[60]

Whitman does not reject moral values; what he does reject is
the hierarchy of moral values. Evil he accepts as a part of
reality. What he strenuously opposed was the ignoring of evil,
and the categorizing of evil. Life to Whitman was equally
divine in all its forms, he delighted in real, pure existence.
He stresses the worth of everything and everyone and "the
absolute equality in worth of every real existing being."[61]

The part evil plays in Whitman's thought is further clarified
by his idea of "prudence." This is not to be confused with the
Aristotelian concept of moderation in one's actions, but is
similar to the Hindu *karma*, a universal law of cause and effect.
There is a consequence to each of our acts, good or bad, in the
eternal count. The Hindu tries to break the chain of karma and
transcend it to the mystical state of Brahma.

The Bhagavad-Gita gives us a religion by which the rule of
karma, the natural order of deed and consequence, can be
transcended. There is no element of caprices or arbitrary
interference of a transcendent purpose within the natural
order. The teacher of the Gita recognizes a realm of reality
where karma does not operate and if we establish our rela-

tions with it, we are free in our deepest being. The chain of karma can be broken here and now, within the flux of the empirical world. We become masters of karma by developing detachment and faith in God.[62]

But Whitman, as did Emerson, took from the Hindu Scriptures only those ideas which helped him formulate his own thoughts. Whitman especially did not seek to transcend the physical world and escape the law of karma. What probably appealed to both Whitman and Emerson was that the law of karma was a *natural* rather than a supernatural explanation of morality. Emerson's idea of "Compensation" is similar to Whitman's "prudence," as will be pointed out. In "Poem of the Sayers of the Words of the Earth," Whitman says, "The song is to the singer and comes back most to him," or, in other words, a person is held in account for each act he commits. This is an early expression of the idea taken from the 1856 edition of *Leaves of Grass*:

> Each man to himself, and each woman to herself, is the
>   word of the past and present, and the word of im-
>   mortality,
> Not one can acquire for another—not one!
> Not one can grow for another—not one![63]

In "Song of Prudence" Whitman sets forth his doctrine in more detail. He places "Prudence" on the same level as his thoughts on Time, Space and Reality, and then explains:

> The Soul is of itself,
> All verges to it, all has reference to what ensues,
> All that a person does, says, thinks, is of consequence,
> Not a move can a man or a woman make, that affects him
>   or her in a day, month, any part of the direct lifetime,
>   or the hour of death,
> But the same affects him or her onward afterward through
>   the indirect lifetime.[64]

Again, Whitman never lets us forget that he views everything not from our present state of existence, but from the vantage point of eternity. He links all causes and effects through the endless cycle of birth and death. It is difficult to think of any aspect of his thought without relating it to the whole. He says, "Not the word or deed ... but has results beyond death, as really as before death." As far as rewards are concerned, "Who has been wise receives interest," if not in the present then at some future stage in the souls journey ("all will come round"). And "not one word or deed" of those who involve themselves in "betrayal, murder, seduction, prostitution," will go unanswered.

This doctrine of karma, or pantheistic determinism should not be confused with the Christian belief in the retribution of sins. Whitman makes no distinctions or judgments; he refuses to classify people into categories of good or bad. Prudence is indivisible, it

> Declines to separate one part of life from every part,
> Divides not the righteous from the unrighteous, or the living
>   from the dead. . . .[65]

Whitman would deny any code of conduct imposed upon the individual by the claim of divine revelation. No institution, no matter what its claims, can teach the individual how to live virtuously.

> No specification is necessary, all that a male or female does,
>   that is vigorous, benevolent, clean, is so much profit
>   to him or her,
> In the unshakable order of the universe, and through the
>   whole scope of it forever.[66]

The soul, therefore, "revolts from every lesson but its own."[67] To the question, "What is the standard of right conduct?" Whitman's answer can be disturbing—"Whatever satisfies the soul is true."[68] But the poet's most abiding belief is that the intuitive knowledge of the soul leads to love of all the creation, sympathy with all creatures, bodily health, and the promotion of happiness in one's self and others."[69]

There are similarities between Whitman and Emerson's thoughts on morality. Both rejected a morality based on external authority, and asserted that the individual soul was the only basis for moral truth. Emerson said that all things are moral, and the "soul which within us is a sentiment, outside us is a law." Thus if man attunes himself to the same law which is within him and the creation, he will always be following the good. In addition since a "perfect equity adjusts its balance in all parts of life," justice is not postponed; for "every crime is punished, every virtue rewarded, every wrong redressed in silence and certainty."[70] However, Emerson differs from Whitman in claiming that justice takes place in our present state of existence only. Thus, in his essay "Prudence," Emerson writes:

> Prudence concerns the *present time* [italics mine], persons, property and existing forms.[71]

Whitman would not limit the consequences for our actions to this life only but to the soul's eternal evolutionary cycles.

As has been mentioned before, Whitman's thought did not develop amid the long-standing conflict of New England religious sects, as did that of Parker and Emerson. Nevertheless scattered throughout his writings there are sufficient statements to establish his position via historical Christianity. To begin with, he echoes Emerson's strong individualism and distrust of authority in the following:

> Stop this day and night with me and you shall possess
> the origin of all poems; . . .
> You shall no longer take things at second or third hand,
> nor look through the eyes of the dead, nor feed on the
> spectres in books,
> You shall not look through my eyes either, not take things
> from me,
> You shall listen to all sides and filter them from your-
> self.[72]

And as far as the current churches are concerned:

> Not all the traditions can put vitality in churches,
> They are not alive, they are cold mortar and brick, . . .[73]

He opposes, as did the deists and transcendentalists, the exclusive claims of religion of possessing divine truth. Each man contains within him all that is needed to make him one with God.

He needs no divine mediator, or book of sacred scriptures to
guide his life.

> Thee (Spiritual Democracy) in all-supplying, all-enclosing
>   worship—thee in no single bible saviour, merely,
> Thy saviours countless, latent within thyself, thy bibles
>   incessant within thyself, equal to any, divine as any.[74]

He remarks on the meaninglessness for him of the conventional
idea of heaven and hell.

> And the threat of what is call'd hell is little
>   or nothing to me,
> And the lure of what is call'd heaven is little
>   or nothing to me; . . .[75]

For both are contained within him, within everyman:

> The pleasures of heaven are with me and the pains of
>   hell are with me,
> The first I graft and increase upon myself, the latter I
>   translate into a new tongue.[76]

Whitman voices his opposition to the traditional account of
revelation and miracles, as did his precursors in natural religion.
He considers "a curl of smoke or a hair on the back of my hand
just as curious as any revelation."[77] In his poem "Miracles,"
he asserts his abiding belief that the creation itself is the
only and greatest of miracles. "Why, who makes much of a
miracle?" The poet knows nothing else but miracles, . . . "To me
every hour of the light and dark is a miracle,/Every cubic inch
of space is a miracle,/Every square yard of the surface of the
earth is spread with the same,/Every foot of the interior swarms
with the same."[78]

He refers to the futility of thinking in logical terms about
God, and reveals his impatience with theologians when he says,
"Be not curious about God,/For I who am curious about each am
not curious about God,/(No array of terms can say how much I
am at peace about God . . .)" Like mystics in general, Whitman
renounces metaphysical speculation and theology for direct

emotional experience and intuition. God, of course, for Whitman is not to be conceived of in the traditional sense, but is actually a realization of cosmic evolution. Thus, he can write, "I only am he who places over you no master, owner, better God, beyond what waits intrinsically in Yourself."[79] And since he believed in the evolutionary migrations of the soul through all forms of life, Whitman can declare, "I am myself waiting my time to be a God."[80]

In the following excerpt he sees himself as a new religious teacher (though there have been many in the past, there will be others in the future).

> I too, following many and follow'd by many, inaugurate a
>   religion, I descend into the arena, . . .[81]

His religion is not to be organized nor institutionalized, for, he declares, "I have no chair, no church, no philosophy. . . . But each man and each woman of you I lead upon a knoll."[82] It is wrong to believe in a particular church or philosophy, according to Whitman, because truth cannot be pinned down in propositions. "All truths wait in all things . . . Logic and sermons never convince"[83] because the universe is forever evolving to new situations in which new truths must be developed. Thus, he says, "All religion, all solid things, . . . all that was or is apparent upon this globe or any globe, falls into niches and corners before the procession of souls along the grand roads of the universe."[84] This means that all established institutions, religion included, are destined to become outmoded, and to be replaced by new ones, in the course of evolution. It is the purpose of America to remold and replace these institutions, for she represents the highest stage thus far in the soul's procession through time.

> Brain of the New World what task is thine,
> To formulate the modern . . .
> Out of thyself, comprising science, to recast
>   poems, churches, art,
> (Recast, maybe discard them, end them—maybe
>   their work is done, who knows?)[85]

The above discussion casts considerable light upon Whitman's seemingly self-contradictory statement, that he is "neither for nor against institutions." Institutions are to be taken pragmatically for the specific condition in the evolutionary process. If they are no longer suitable, they should be abolished, or at least modified to fit the present state of things. All in all, however, Whitman seems to be more against than for institutions. Not only was he inclined to this view because of the Quakers' preference for the inner light, but it was also his firm faith that imperfections will be meliorated with time.

Whitman's religion is the same as his philosophy, and his philosophy is his religion. This is true because his mystical pantheism is all-embracing and makes no separation of knowledge into different categories. Thus, he could say, "Hurrah for positive science," in one moment, and the next moment commune with his soul in divine ecstasy. Science has as much to do with the soul, as the soul's pantheistic identification with all things. We could say that science proves the existence of the soul, in Whitman's view, as does his direct intuition of it. For

Clear and sweet is my soul, and clear and sweet is all that
    is not my soul.
Lack one lacks both, and the unseen is proved by the
    seen,
Till that becomes unseen and receives proof in its turn.[86]

Since his pantheism views the creation as constantly unfolding to the central perfection of the soul, all earlier expressions of religion are absorbed into the present, and each in its turn has added to and developed the knowledge of that which came before. And the future will lead to even greater and more complete religious expressions. This idea of evolutionary religious concepts is not a new one; we have seen that it was an inherent part of Parker and Emerson's natural religion. It matters not whether Whitman got it from them or not, for it is a natural outcome of his own evolutionary pantheistic philosophy. Whitman explains the idea through "identification." The poet feels within him all the old gods and mythical figures. His journeying soul is present at their birth, their sufferings, their deaths.

Taking myself the exact dimensions of Jehovah,
Lithographing Kronos, Zeus his son, and Hercules his
  grandson,
Buying drafts of Osiris, Isis, Belus, Brahma, Buddha,
In my portfolio placing Manito loose, Allah on a leaf, the
  crucifix engraved,
With Odin and the hideous-faced Mexitili and every idol
  and image
Taking them all for what they are worth and not a cent
  more,
Admitting they were alive and did the work of their days,
(They bore mites as for unfledg'd birds who have now to
  rise and fly and sing for themselves,)
*Accepting the rough deific sketches to fill out better in
  myself*, bestowing them freely on each man and woman
  I see, ...[87]

In another section of "Song of Myself," his list includes the
"gospels" and "him that was crucified." Whitman makes no differ-
entiation between the so-called "higher" religions and the primitive religions. Nor, for that matter, between believers and
atheists.

I do not despise you priests, all time, the world over,
My faith is the greatest of faiths and the least of faiths,
Enclosing worship ancient and modern and all between
  ancient and modern,
Believing I shall come again upon the earth after five
  thousand years,
Waiting responses from oracles, honoring the gods, saluting
  the sun,
Making a fetich of the first rock or stump, powowing with
  sticks in the circle of obis,
Helping the llama or brahmin as he trims the lamps of
  the idols,
Dancing yet through the streets in a phallic procession, rapt
  and austere in the woods a gymnosophist,
Drinking mead from the skull-cap, to Shastas and Vedas
  admirant, miding the Koran,
Walking the teokallis, spotted with gore from the stone and
  knife, beating the serpent-skin drum,

Accepting the Gospels, accepting him that was crucified,
  knowing assuredly that he is divine,
To the mass kneeling or the puritan's prayer rising, or sitting
  patiently in a pew, ...
Down-hearted doubters dull and excluded,
Frivolous, sullen, moping, angry, affected, dishearten'd,
  atheistical,
I know every one of you, I know the sea of torment, doubt,
  despair and unbelief.[88]

As Whitman explains, his faith is the "greatest of faiths" because he embraces the whole history of religious thought, and it is "the least of faiths" because he does not accept any specific creed as the ultimate answer, and even includes the doubters and the atheists within his religious scheme.

In "Chanting The Square Deific," Whitman attempts to give symbolic form to his cosmic pantheism by creating a new Godhead. To the old pantheon of pagan and Christian gods, he adds his own, "Santa Spirita," a deity which seems to be very much like the pantheistic "I" of his other poems. In addition, Sixbey says that Whitman sought to fuse both Eastern and Western ideas in this poem, as indeed, he attempted to do in his poetry in general.

I see that the world of the West, as part of all fuses inseparably with the East, and with all as time does—the ever new, yet old, old, human race—"the same subject continued," as the novels of our grandfathers had it for chapter heads. If we are not to hospitably receive and complete and complete the inauguration of the old civilizations and change their small scale to the largest, broadest scale, what on earth are we for?[89]

"Chanting The Square Deific" is composed of four stanzas, each of which describes one side of the quaternity and suggests its attributes. The poem is organized similarly to the Apostles' and Nicene Creeds in which each successive paragraph treats the qualities of one of the persons of the Trinity.[90] The first side of the Deific Square represents law and judgment. Whitman lists here the masculine deities, Brahma, Jehovah, Saturn, Kronos.

"I dispense from this side judgment, inexorable without the least remorse."[91] In the next stanza Whitman depicts the consolators as the second side of the quaternity. One is surprised to find Hermes listed along with Christ. In explanation, Sixbey says, "Like Christ, the Good Shepherd Hermes is associated with the protection of cattle and sheep. He is also the messenger of the gods and conductor of souls sent to the underworld. But Whitman's chief reason for including Hermes is indicated in his comment in his list of Gods: "(Mercury) Hermes, the God of Science." For science, Whitman believed, was one of the sure roads to progress, democracy, and perfection.[92]

Hercules seems to be out of place with Christ and Hermes. Whitman was probably thinking of the labors of Hercules, of his sorrow and suffering. At any rate, Christ and his two pagan associates comprise the second side of the Square, representing love and consolation.

For I am affection, I am the cheer-bringing God, with hope and all enclosing charity.[93]

In the third stanza appears the principle of revolt in the figure of Satan, "with sudra face and worn brow, black, but in the depths of my heart, proud as any."[94] Satan opposes both the first side—the rigid pattern of law and conventional morality, and the universal affection of the "cheer-bringing God." The inclusion of this figure in the Godhead was the product of years of reflection on Whitman's part. As has been discussed previously, Whitman conceived of evil as a necessary ingredient in the process of cosmic evolution. Rebellion and revolt, are therefore positive and contribute toward the development of man and nature. In *Notes and Fragments* under "Theories of Evil," Whitman lists *"Faust, Manfred, Paradise Lost, Book of Job."*[95]

Thus, the Satan of "Chanting The Square Deific" is not simply a negative force opposing law and consolation in the universe. "Rather, he is a positive stimulus to the self respect, or in Whitman's language, to the identity of the individual. In the political state, this Satan leads not to anarchy, but to freedom from the tyranny of legalism. Even in religion Satan would exert a constructive force, for no religion in which he is a person [sic] in the Godhead can degenerate into hollow dogma or priestly ritual."[96]

The fourth side of the divine quaternity has occasioned much discussion among critics. Sixbey disagrees with those who claim that Whitman meant his Godhead to represent the Christian Trinity with Satan added. It would then seem likely, Sixbey argues, that he would have named the remaining person "Holy Ghost or Holy Spirit." "His use of what would be the feminine form of the Italian *Santo Spirito* suggests that he may have conceived this side of the *Square Deific* as being different from the Holy Ghost; . . . the feminine form of the name is significant."[97] Throughout his writings Whitman exalted the idea of motherhood, as in his own life he dearly loved and venerated his mother. Sixbey interprets *Santa Spirita* as "the spirit of America as Whitman conceived America to be. Her inclusive sympathy replaces that of the Virgin Mary, as it was popularly understood during the Middle Ages."[98] Such a love, Whitman felt, existed universally—"it waits and has always been waiting, latent in all men." [To the East and To the West.] It is the pure, tender affection which is at the base of "the institution of the dear love of comrades" that Whitman sought to establish everywhere. *Santa Spirita* is

breather, life
Beyond the light, lighter than light . . .
Including all life on earth, touching,
    including God, including Saviour and Satan . . .[99]

Thus, the apparent conflicts among the first three sides—law, consolation and revolt—which develop a masculine hierarchy, are mystically resolved by *Santa Spirita* through all-inclusive love.

A discussion of Whitman's religion would be incomplete if it did not include his idea of Personalism. "Whitman gave the title 'Personalism' to the essay which became the nucleus of 'Democratic Vistas,' and used it to designate the fusion of the in-

dividual with the mass in an ideal democracy of the future."[100]
However, he never clearly defined the term and further elucida-
tion is necessary in order to understand him completely on this
point. The following passage is an example of the difficulty
one is confronted with.

The ripeness of religion is doubtless to be looked for
in this field of individuality, and is a result that no organiza-
tion or church can ever achieve. As history is poorly retain'd
by what the technists call history, and is not given out from
their pages, except the learner has in himself the sense
of the well-wrapt, never yet written, perhaps impossible to
be written, history—so Religion, although casually arrested,
and, after a fashion, preserv'd in the churches and creeds,
does not depend at all upon them, but is a part of the
identified soul, which, when greatest, knows not bibles in
the old way, but in new ways—the identified soul, which
can really confront Religion when it extricates itself entirely
from the churches, and not before.
Personalism fuses this, and favors it. I should say, indeed,
that only in the perfect uncontamination and solitariness
of individuality may the spirituality of religion positively
come forth at all. Only here, and on such terms, the media-
tion, the devout ecstasy, the soaring flight. Only here, communion with the mysteries, the eternal problems, whence?
whither? Alone, and identity, and the mood—and the soul
emerges, and all statements, churches, sermons, melt away
like vapors. Alone, and silent thought and awe, and aspira-
tion—and then the interior consciousness, like a hitherto
unseen inscription, in magic ink, beams out its wondrous
lines to the sense. Bibles may convey, and priests expound,
but is exclusively for the noiseless operation of one's isolated
Self, to enter the pure ether of veneration, reach the divine
levels, and commune with the unutterable.[101]

The obscurity of the passage will vanish if one thinks of
it in light of Whitman's mysticism. There are also strong Emer-
sonian overtones. True religion does not exist in churches or
creeds, but within the individual—within the individual who
has an "identified soul." Only he can attain intuitive knowledge

and make contact with the Divine. Professor Allen describes
the term "identified soul" as follows:

> at physiological birth each body receives its "identity,"
> meaning that a "soul" is assigned to it so that each exists
> through the other. Or we might say that the soul has be-
> come individual. In other words, individuality and per-
> sonality depend ultimately upon *soul* and *spirit*. Here we
> come to the crux of the problem of the relationship between
> individuality and universality, or atomic multiplicity and
> the pantheistic One, or man and God. Whitman says that
> Personalism "fuses," and as we shall see presently, he
> means by this that the doctrine resolves the problem, on
> the one hand, of individualism versus society, or on the
> other hand, of man versus God or "Over-Soul."[102]

It is in Alcott's use of the term that we can gain a clearer
idea of what Whitman means by "Personalism." Alcott knew
Whitman as a friend, and was even more drawn to him by
receipt of the essay on "Personalism."[103] Incidentally the essay
seems to have aided Alcott in formulating his own theories on
the subject; so it seems likely that he, if anyone did, understood
Whitman's doctrine. In 1868, the year Alcott received Whitman's
essay, he wrote the following in a letter:

> The unity of the Personality; the difference is the Individual-
> ity. . . . We must grow into and become one with the Person
> dwelling in every breast, and thus come to apprehend the
> saying "I and my Father are one"—that is, to perceive that
> all souls have a Personal identity with God and abide
> in him.[104]

The definition sounds very much like Christian mysticism, but
the idea that "all souls have a Personal identity with God,"
could also be read in terms of Whitman's pantheism, which
asserts that man and God are one.

A fuller discussion of Alcott's concept is the following from
his *Journal*, for May 17, 1874:

> The Person is the pre-supposition of all things and beings.
> Nothing were without this premise. I am because God
> is; nor am I found save by his Presence in my consciousness,

and incarnation therefrom. From my soul spring forth my
senses, reflecting itself in natural images. My body is my
mind's idol. From the beginning I was, and survive all
things beside myself. Personally immortal, time deals my
periods and dates me by its revolutions. I am born and
die daily.

> Would'st know thyself and all things see?
> Become thyself, and all things be.

> Now, now, thy knowing is too slow.
> Thought is the knowing in the now.

> Depose thyself if thou would'st be
> Drest in fresh suit of deity.

> Out of the chaos rose in sight
> One globe's fair form in living light.

> Were God not God, I were not I,
> Myself in him I must descry.[105]

Here, as in Whitman's pantheism, we are shown the intimate relationship of man and God. This union is manifested in Personality; that is, man's personality is immortalized in the personality of God. The "identified soul" of Whitman can be translated
into Alcott's "Become thyself, and all things be." This doctrine
emphasizes self-reliance, but not as means of becoming individual, but as a means of realizing the divine personality
within the individual soul, so that by developing its full potential
the soul becomes closer to God or the pantheistic All. "Thus
Personalism curbs and directs Whitman's earlier extreme individualism into ethical and religiously unselfish channels."[106]

Although this doctrine of doing away with selfishness by
consciously merging the individual self with the Great Self
or Soul resembles pantheism, personalism and pantheism retain
some differences. We note these differences by contrasting the
ideas of Emerson with those of Alcott and Whitman. Emerson, in
denying any personality to God, in favor of a superpersonal
creator, was thus more pantheistic than Whitman (in 1868).
Opponents of pantheism come from two sources: one, theism,

which is critical of it because it denies that God is a person,[107] and two, believers in personalism, who, like Alcott, objected to pantheism because it tends to promote excessive individualism, by denying personality to the soul and to God.

Whitman used the term "Personalism" in "Democratic Vistas" for his political theory, and he was at the time not concerned with its theological implications as was Alcott.[108] However, in his pantheism Whitman had always asserted that the individual by identifying his soul with all things experienced the Divine Essence itself. "For this reason there is no great theological contradiction between Whitman's earlier, intense pantheism and his later Personalism."[109] Early, in *Notes and Fragments* he said, "I know that Personality is divine and gives life and identity to a man or woman."[110] Further along he reflects, "behind all the faculties of the human being, as the sight, and other senses, and ever the emotions and the intellect stands the real power, the mystical identity, the real I or Me, or You."[111] In "Carol of Occupations" (1855) he proclaims that the only reality is persons, not things, and that "you and your soul enclose all things."[112]

This insistence that all reality is a pantheistic personality from which individual souls have sprung and in which they find their unity, is basically not individualistic, and never was in Whitman's thought. He had merely emphasized the potentialities of his own self—or soul—and thereby the possible development of other individuals, as a means of stimulating them to growth, expression, and the achievement of their innate divinity. The Personalism of "Democratic Vistas," therefore, is not a new and contradictory idea in Whitman's thought, but a synthesis of his original doctrines of the divinity of the Self, the cosmic equality of all Souls, and their complete unity in a common immortality.[113]

For it is only by the interdependence of the Me and the Not-Me that the full realization of the individual is possible. Whitman states this thought most memorably in the famous lines:

One's-self I sing, a simple separate person,
Yet utter the word Democratic, the word En-Masse.[114]

In "Democratic Vistas," his major prose work, Whitman explains in more detail the problem of the individual and society.

This idea of perfect individualism it is indeed that which deepest tinges and gives character to the idea of the aggregate. For it is mainly or altogether to serve independent separation, that we favor a strong generalization, consolidation. As it is to give the best vitality and freedom to the right of the states (every bit as important as the right of nationality, the union), that we insist on the identity of the Union at all hazards.[115]

The analogy that Whitman makes of the states and the Union is merely a transposing onto the political level of the relationship between the Self and the pantheistic All. As the divine purpose is best fulfilled by the utmost development of the individual soul, likewise in society the best interests of the aggregate is provided for and attained by the development of individual personality and moral character. "Produce great Persons the rest follows."[116] The important thing "towering above all talk and argument. . . . the last-needed proof of democracy, . . . its personalities."[117]

Whitman's religion is humanistic—in the place of the institutionalized religions, he would substitute a religion based on the divinity of the common man. In language reminiscent of the deists and transcendentalists Whitman claims that in the unfolding of the divine plan the existing formal creeds will wither away.

There will soon be no more priests. Their work is done. They may wait awhile—perhaps a generation or two—dropping off by degrees. A superior breed shall take their place—the gangs of the Kosmos and prophets en masse shall take their place. A new order shall arise and they shall be the priests of man, and every man shall be his own priest. The churches built under their umbrage shall be the churches of men and women. Through the divinity of themselves shall the Kosmos and the new breed of poets be interpreters of men and women and of all events and things. They shall find their inspiration in real objects today, symptoms of the past and future—They shall arise in America and be responded to from the remainder of the earth.[118]

Democracy, then, as Whitman conceived of it, was not merely a political but a religious ideal. "For I say at the core of democracy finally, is the religious element which ever seeks to bind, all nations, all men, of however various and distant lands, into a brotherhood, a family."[119] This spiritual democracy is based on two principles: the divine worth of the individual and the equality of individuals brought together not through law, but by the bonds of love.

It is the old, yet, ever-modern dream of earth, out of her eldest and her youngest, her fond philosophers and poets. Not that half only, individualism which isolates, there is another half, which is adhesiveness or love, that fuses, ties, and aggregates, making the races comrades, and fraternizing all. Both are to be vitalized by religion (sole worthiest elevator of man or State) breathing into the proud material tissues, the breath of life.[120]

Whitman occasionally used the term "adhesiveness," which he got from the current pseudo-science, phrenology. But the term which is more typically his is the "dear love of comrades." It was the means by which Whitman's ideal of universal brotherhood was to be realized: "divine magnetic lands with the love of comrades with the life-long love of comrades."[121] Speaking psychologically, one could say the doctrine is the "Calamus emotion," uplifted, universalized, and informed with spirit. At any rate, Whitman exhalted the "institution of the dear love of comrades" as his program for bringing into being a spiritual democracy and a world community of nations. For Whitman felt that if he could know men of different countries "I should become attached to them as I do to men in my own lands."

I have looked for equals and lovers and found them ready for me in all lands,
I think some divine rapport has equalized me with them.[122]

Whitman's emphasis on "the institution of the dear love of comrades" is unique in natural religion, and the most personal aspect of his thought. Emerson's extreme individualism was rarely balanced with any pronounced social thrust. He did, however, offer the suggestion in his essay, "Politics," that "the power of love, as the basis of a State has never been tried."[123] Whitman greatly amplified that thought in his doctrine of adhesiveness as the force binding the individual with the aggregate.

In "Thou Mother with Thy Equal Brood," Whitman glorifies the states of the Union with their various nationalities. Freneau's patriotic fervor in "The Rising Glory of America" is re-echoed by Whitman:

Thou Mother with thy equal brood,
Thou varied chain of different States, yet one identity only.
A special song before I go I'd sing O'er all the rest,
For thee, the future.
I'd sow the seed for thee of endless Nationality.[124]

In "Song of The Redwood Tree" America is viewed as the culmination of cosmic evolutionary process. Standing on the western California shore, the poet meditates upon "the empire new . . . come from Nature's long and harmless throes, peacefully builded. . . ." He contemplates her "average spiritual manhood." Beneath all the vast materials of America is that "unseen moral essence" that "sometimes known, oftener unknown, really shape[s] and mould[s] the New World, adjusting it to Time and Space." Despite all the errors and "perturbations of the surface" and beneath all "creeds, arts, statutes, literatures" this unseen potentiality ("vital, universal, deathless germs") establishes here for good "these areas entire, lands of the Western shore."[125] America then is

The new society at last, proportionate to Nature, . . .
Fresh come to a new world indeed, yet long prepared,
. . . the genius of the modern, child of the real and the ideal,
Clearing the ground for broad humanity, the true America,
    heir of the past so grand,
To build a grander future.[126]

Whitman envisioned America to be not only the highest manifestation of the evolutionary principle in man and nature, but
the precursor of universal brotherhood. As all men within American society are bound by democratic-spiritual ties, so are all
people within other countries similarly bound. This One World
concept is implied in "Song of The Redwood Tree" where America is said to "clear the ground for broad humanity ... to build
a greater future." However, we are given a more explicit presentation of the One World concept in that strangely moving
poem "Sleepers." The image is that of diverse humanity lying
hand in hand around the globe.

> The sleepers that lived and died wait, the far advanced
>   are to go on in their turns, and the far behind are to
>   come on in their turns,
> The diverse shall be no less diverse, but they shall flow
>   and unite—they unite now.
>
> The sleepers are very beautiful as they lie unclothed,
> They flow hand in hand over the whole earth from east to
>   west as they lie unclothed,
> The Asiatic and African are hand in hand, the European
>   and American are hand in hand, ...[127]

The encircling image of international brotherhood appears again
in "Passage to India." The poem, inspired by the opening of the
Suez Canal which afforded an easier passage for circumnaviga-
tion of the globe, in Whitman's hands becomes a glowing eulogy
of the soul's ageless journey through time and space, recording
its progress through the history of all nations and peoples.
America, the highest point in the soul's journey thus far, is
the geographical, cultural and spiritual link binding East and
West, and past with future.

> thou born America,
> For purpose vast, man's long probation fill'd
> Thou rondure of the world at last accomplished.[128]

With Walt Whitman natural religion thus reaches its culmination in American literature. The earlier doctrines and beliefs
of the deists and transcendentalists alike point toward his

affirmative, optimistic faith in the religion of nature and the common man. He follows the deistic reaction against institution-alized religion, and carries on the transcendental idea of re-ligion as constantly evolving to a more perfect expression of the soul. However, he broadened and deepened natural religion by proclaiming the equal divinity of body and soul, and stressed the moral and spiritual equality of all individuals by virtue of their common existence in God (or World Soul). In addition, he evolved the idea of a spiritual democracy, the natural out-growth of his mystical pantheism and his love for the common man.

In his conception of God, Whitman differs somewhat from the deists and transcendentalists. Actually, the Deity is a name for a cosmic evolutionary process, or perhaps a great personality with human personalities existing within Him. Whitman's doc-trine of Personalism brings him closer to Alcott than to either Parker or Emerson.

No one among the advocates of natural religion was so con-fident in proclaiming America to be the highest development, so far, in the evolution of human societies, nor asserted her role to be that of unifier of all nations, creeds, and races. Whit-man's religion is truly universal and all-embracing in its one-world vision.

Conclusion

Throughout its course, natural religion, although differing in emphasis and method, remained consistent in its disregard of miracle and authority in man's relationship to God. For Paine and Allen supernatural revelation was blind superstition which clouded the minds of men and was a hindrance to the promulgation of true religion. The deists condemned the "First Revelation" thoroughly. Paine actually claimed the Bible to be an "evil" book which, in many ways, was disruptive of morality. Jefferson's view was not as extreme, for he saw in the Bible great ethical truths which he gleaned from it by casting out all passages concerned with miracles. Parker's position was transitional; he stood midway between deism and transcendentalism, using for the most part the arguments of the deists and leaning toward, but not fully embracing, Emerson's mystical Brahmanism. In Walt Whitman natural religion reached its fullest nineteenth-century development. His religion of the common man unites the republican religion of the deists with the transcendentalist's communion of the soul with nature.

 The meaning of the term "nature" altered in the evolution of natural religion. The deists viewed nature as an external physical reality which reflected the order and design of the creator. By observing the universal laws by which nature operated, man could apprehend God's wisdom and perfection. Thus they made a distinction between mind and matter; the mind acted upon the things it observed in nature, and from this sense—data drew rational deductions. God was thus deduced from the evidence of order and design in the Creation. The transcendentalists borrowing the epistemology of the German Romantic philosophers, Kant, Fichte and Schelling, tended to blur the distinction between mind and matter. Emerson, using their terminology, said that the understanding was the faculty that proceeded by logic and deduction (reason for the deists), and by reason he meant the "highest faculty of the soul" or intuition. Reason, he felt, was potentially perfect in every man, but understanding varied with the individual. Nature's role in the ascension to divine knowledge was that of mediator; the individual by gazing with the inner eye was thus able to unite the mind with objects in nature. At those moments when the inner and outer worlds were perceived as one, the individual experienced his existence in God, or the Oversoul.

Whitman borrowed a great deal from Emerson. He, too, opposed the rationalism of the deists and stressed the intuition of the transcendentalists. But Whitman's philosophy has a more pronounced sensual and social thrust than Emerson's. Not only nature, but the bond of human relationships were a means of communion with God. Whitman deified the body equally with the soul, and thus infused an emotional and physical quality into the still austere intellectualism of Concord philosophy. Whitman saw democracy not only in his own society, but in the cosmos. He glorified equally every particle of matter, every globule of life, every inch of space. His method was not, like Emerson's, an act of perception, but an act of all-embracing love.

Viewed culturally, natural religion evolved out of the need to formulate a new relationship between man, God and nature based on the realities and novelty of American experience, since the traditional faith no longer fulfilled those needs. The dominant ideals of that new experience were: individual freedom, distrust of authority, and the equality of all men before their Creator. Natural religion appears in American literature as an expression of those ideals.

Our method has been largely comparative; by setting off deistic and transcendental concepts against those of historical Christianity, we were able to define their outlines more clearly than would have been possible if a straight descriptive method were followed. By so doing, Matthiessen's delineation of two streams in American literature appears very clearly and distinctly. Such figures as Hawthorne, James, Eliot and Faulkner embody in their writings the more traditional Christian viewpoint. Unlike the advocates of natural religion, they show the conflict between good and evil, have a more pessimistic view of human nature, and dramatize the role of suffering in the purification of the self.

Epilogue

The history of natural religion does not end with Walt Whitman, but continues to play a vital role in American literature up to the present time. The fervent optimism of natural religion, however, was considerably tempered by the Civil War. Whitman in particular reflects some of this disillusionment in "Democratic Vistas" (1871).

A link between the transcendental expression of natural religion and the later naturalists is Oliver Wendell Holmes's *Mechanism In Thoughts and Morals*. In this work Holmes discusses the influence of scientific determinism on morality and makes a strong stand for human responsibility. Holmes is actually opposed to any kind of determinism, whether scientific or Calvinist. He echoes the deistic arguments of Paine and Ethan Allen when he says, "If a created being has no right which his creator is bound to respect, there is an end to all moral relations between them."[1] Deploring the excessive veneration of the Judaic-Christian tradition, Holmes in a whimsical manner states one of the basic themes of this study: "Though our rocky New England and old rocky Judaea always seem to have a kind of yearning for each other. . . . political freedom inevitably generates a new type of religious character."[2]

In the writings of the naturalists man is stripped of his transcendental nobility and is depicted as an isolated being pitted against the vast and pervasive power of nature. For example, in Frank Norris' *The Octopus*, nature ceases to be the reflection of the Oversoul, and is viewed as a potent energy

169

possessing almost a life of its own. In one of his numerous descriptions of the growing of the wheat Norris says the following:

> One could not take a dozen steps ... without the brusque sensation that underfoot the land was alive; aroused at last from its sleep, palpitating with the desire of reproduction. Deep down in the recesses of the soil, the great heart throbbed once more, ... vibrating with desire, offering itself to the caress of the plough, insistent, eager, imperious.[3]

And amidst the vast indifference of cosmic forces, man is reduced to insignificance.

> What were these heated, tiny squabbles, this feverish, small bustle of mankind, this minute swarming of the human insect, to the great, majestic, silent ocean of the Wheat itself! Indifferent, gigantic, resistless, it moved in its appointed grooves. Men. [sic] Lilliputians, gnats in the sunshine, buzzed impudently in their tiny battles, were born, lived through their little day, died, and were forgotten; while the Wheat wrapped in Nirvanic calm, grew steadily under the night, alone with the stars and with God.[4]

Norris' primitive animism is further developed by John Steinbeck in *To a God Unknown*. In this novel of a poor farmer who stubbornly refuses to give up his sterile land, the relationship of man to nature is enacted through such pagan rituals as libations of meat and wine, and tree worship. Steinbeck also makes use of the "Myth of The Fisher King," in which the fertility of the land is bound up with the health and well-being of the land owner. In the end the former sacrifices his own life so that the land may become fertile. The conflict between Steinbeck's natural religion and historical Christianity is dramatized by the arguments between the protagonist and a Catholic priest who tries to persuade the farmer to renounce his "corrupt" paganism. Steinbeck seems to indicate in this novel that it is necessary that man regain this "ancient knowledge" long suppressed by the Church.

In his later novel, *The Grapes of Wrath*, Steinbeck modifies the extreme primitivism of *To a God Unknown*. Emersonianism and the Whitmanesque compassion for the common man re-appear in the character of Jim Casey, the self-styled Okie preacher. Unorthodox Jim Casey went to the wilderness to find himself, and it was there that he experienced the religious feeling of identity with nature: "there was the hills, an' there was me, an we wasn't separate no more. We was one thing and that one thing was holy."⁵ At another point in the novel Jim says: "Maybe it's all men, and all women we love; maybe that's the Holy Spirit—the human spirit—the whole shebang. Maybe all men got one big soul ev'bodies a part of."⁶ Throughout his writings Steinbeck believes in the spontaneous goodness of simple folk who are closely related to the soil, and reveals a radical distrust of conventional piety and morality.

In *The Ox-Bow Incident*, Davies, the idealist whose conscience is troubled as a result of his inability to stop the lynching, ex-pounds deistic and transcendental arguments when he says: the individual's sense of justice is a higher authority than the law.

> None of man's Temples, none of his religions . . . his arts, his sciences, nothing else he has grown to is so great a thing as . . . his justice, this sense of justice is the true law—is something in itself; it is the spirit of the moral nature of man; it is an existence apart like God, and as worthy of worship as God. If we can touch God at all, where do we touch him save in the conscience? And what is the con-science of any man save his little fragment of the conscience of all men in all time?⁷

One of the most representative exponents of natural religion in contemporary poetry is Wallace Stevens. In "Sunday Morning," Stevens is critical of historical Christianity and seems to maintain that divinity must be centered in sensuous, emotional experience, not traditional heavenly modes. At the beginning of the poem, the central figure, a woman, is portrayed seated in a chair in her sunlit parlor, musing:

> Why should she give her bounty to the dead?
> What is divinity if it can come
> Only in silent shadows and in dreams?

Shall she not find in comforts of the sun,
In pungent fruit and bright, green wings, or else
In any balm or beauty of the earth,
Things to be cherished like the thought of heaven?
Divinity must live within herself:
Passions of rains, or moods in falling snow;
Grievings in loneliness, or unsubdued
Elations when the forest blooms; gusty
Emotions on wet roads on autumn nights;
All pleasures and all pains, remembering
The bough of summer and the winter branch.
These are the measures destined for her soul.[8]

Thus, this brief glimpse indicates that natural religion in current American literature is a rich vein still to be explored.

Notes and References

Introduction

1. Cecil Moore, *English Prose of the Eighteenth Century*, (New York, 1933), p. 356.
2. *Ibid.*
3. Basil Willey, *The Seventeenth Century Background* (New York, 1953), p. 128.
4. *Ibid.*
5. *Ibid.*
6. *Ibid.*
7. *Ibid.*, p. 130.
8. *Ibid.*
9. *Ibid.*, p. 131.
10. *Ibid.*
11. *Ibid.*
12. *Ibid.*, pp. 131, 132.
13. *Ibid.*, p. 134.
14. *Ibid.*, p. 135.
15. *Ibid.*
16. *Ibid.*, p. 136.
17. *Ibid.*
18. *Ibid.*, p. 137.
19. *Ibid.*
20. Moore, p. 355.
21. *Ibid.*, p. 356.
22. *Ibid.*
23. Moore, p. 394.
24. Moore, p. 356.
25. *Ibid.*, p. 357.
26. *Ibid.*
27. *Ibid.*
28. *Ibid.*

Chapter One

1. Herbert M. Morais, *Deism in Eighteenth Century America* (New York, 1934), p. 101.
2. Ethan Allen, *Reason, The Only Oracle of Man* (New York, 1836), p. 24.
3. *Ibid.*
4. *Ibid.*
5. *Ibid.*, p. 32.
6. *Ibid.*, p. 37.
7. *Ibid.*, p. 49.
8. *Ibid.*, p. 39.
9. *Ibid.*, p. 43.
10. *Ibid.*, p. 26.
11. *Ibid.*, p. 238.
12. *Ibid.*
13. Morais, p. 13.
14. *Ibid.*
15. Allen, p. 466.
16. Morais, p. 17.
17. Allen, pp. 186, 187.
18. *Ibid.*, p. 200.
19. *Ibid.*, p. 206.
20. *Ibid.*
21. *Ibid.*, p. 194.
22. *Ibid.*
23. *Ibid.*, p. 195.
24. *Ibid.*, p. 196.
25. *Ibid.*, p. 187.
26. *Ibid.*, pp. 186, 187.
27. *Ibid.*, pp. 187, 188.
28. *Ibid.*, p. 192.
29. *Ibid.*
30. *Ibid.*, p. 193.
31. *Ibid.*
32. *Ibid.*, p. 183.
33. *Ibid.*, p. 91.
34. *Ibid.*, p. 112.
35. *Ibid.*, p. 104.
36. *Ibid.*, p. 105.
37. *Ibid.*, pp. 97, 98.
38. *Ibid.*, p. 233.
39. *Ibid.*, p. 235.
40. *Ibid.*
41. *Ibid.*, p. 268.

42. *Ibid.*, p. 411.
43. *Ibid.*, p. 412.
44. *Ibid.*, p. 167.
45. *Ibid.*, pp. 168, 172.
46. *Ibid.*, pp. 467, 468.

Chapter Two

1. Herbert M. Morais, *Deism in Eighteenth Century America* (New York, 1934), p. 120.
2. *Ibid.*, p. 121.
3. *Ibid.*
4. *Ibid.*
5. *Ibid.*
6. *Ibid.*, p. 127.
7. Thomas Paine, *The Age of Reason* (Baltimore, no date), p. 5.
8. *Ibid.*, p. 6.
9. *Ibid.*
10. *Ibid.*
11. *Ibid.*, p. 7.
12. *Ibid.*, pp. 7, 8.
13. *Ibid.*
14. *Ibid.*
15. *Ibid.*, p. 9.
16. A. Powell Davies, *The First Christian: A Study of St. Paul and Christian Origins* (New York, 1959).

A. Powell Davies, a Unitarian minister and biblical scholar, is concerned with tracing the development of Christianity as a synthesis of the Roman and Near Eastern mystery religions and current Jewish thought. Frazer, however, doesn't seem to view Christianity with any more religious significance than he views the religions and myths of the countless cultures he examines. "It is indeed a melancholy and in some respects thankless task to strike at the foundation of beliefs in which, ... the hopes and aspirations of humanity through long ages have sought refuge.... Yet sooner or later it is inevitable that the battery of the comparative method should breach these venerable walls" (*The Golden Bough*, "Introduction").
17. *The Age of Reason*, pp. 8, 9.
18. *Ibid.*, pp. 13, 14.
19. *Ibid.*
20. *Ibid.*, p. 34.
21. *Ibid.*, p. 10.
22. *Ibid.*, p. 18.
23. *Ibid.*, p. 16.
24. *Ibid.*, p. 21.

25. Morais, p. 123.
26. *The Age of Reason,* p. 18.
27. *Ibid.,* p. 26.
28. *Ibid.,* pp. 18, 19.
29. *Ibid.,* p. 33.
30. *The Age of Reason,* p. 32.
31. *Ibid.,* pp. 32, 33.
32. *Ibid.*
33. *Ibid.,* p. 49.
34. *Ibid.,* p. 45.
35. *Ibid.,* p. 57.
36. *Ibid.,* p. 30.
37. *Ibid.,* p. 16.
38. *Ibid.,* p. 35.
39. *Ibid.,* p. 60.
40. *Ibid.,* p. 28.
41. *Ibid.*
42. *Ibid.,* p. 63.
43. *Ibid.,* p. 67.
44. *Ibid.,* p. 58.
45. Cf. Parker, Chap. V., p. 22; Emerson, Chap. VI, p. 40.
46. *The Age of Reason,* p. 68.

Chapter Three

1. Morais, p. 116.
2. There is some disagreement over which writers exerted the most influence on Jefferson. Both I. W. Riley and H. S. Randall (Randall, *Life of Thomas Jefferson,* 1868, N. Y.; Riley, *American Philosophy,* N. Y., 1907) contend that Priestley, the English Unitarian, had a strong influence upon Jefferson's religious views. According to Gilbert Chinard and Karl Lehrmann, the Greek Stoic philosophers played a more influential role.
3. Jefferson, *Writings,* ed. Ford, Vol. VIII, p. 225, quoted in Morais, p. 117.
4. Karl Lehmann, *Thomas Jefferson, American Humanist* (New York, 1947), pp. 42-44.
5. *Ibid.,* p. 433.
6. *The Life and Selected Writings of Thomas Jefferson,* ed. Adrienne Koch and William Peden (New York, 1944), p. 433.
7. *Ibid.,* p. 567.
8. These two terms were sometimes used interchangeably by the deists. Jefferson liked to call the original preachings of Christ deistic; Paine referred to Adam as being born a deist. Morais says that the

term was first used by T. Morgan, an English deist (*The Moral Philosopher*, 1737).

9. *Selected Writings of Jefferson*, p. 569.

10. John Dewey, *The Living Thoughts of Jefferson* (Philadelphia, 1940), p. 93.

11. *The Selected Writings*, p. 706.

12. *Ibid.*, pp. 703, 704.

13. John Dewey, pp. 94, 95.

14. *Ibid.*, p. 570.

15. *Ibid.*, p. 430.

16. *Ibid.*

17. *The Selected Writings*, p. 431.

18. *Ibid.*

19. *The Selected Writings*, p. 313.

Chapter Four

1. Nelson F. Adkins, *Philip Freneau and the Cosmic Enigma* (New York, 1949), p. 56.

2. *The Poems of Freneau*, ed. Harry H. Clark (New York, 1929), p. 422.

3. *Ibid.*, p. 424.

4. *Ibid.*, pp. 424, 425.

5. Lewis Leary, *That Rascal Freneau* (Rutgers University Press, 1941), p. 278.

6. *Ibid.*

7. *Ibid.*

8. *Ibid.*, p. 281.

9. *Ibid.*

10. *Ibid.*, p. 282.

11. *Ibid.*

12. "A New Age of Truth Triumphant," quoted in Adkins, p. 47.

13. *Ibid.*

14. *The Poems of Freneau*, p. 46.

15. Adkins, p. 46.

16. *Ibid.*, p. 45.

17. *Ibid.*, p. 46.

18. *Poems of Freneau*, p. 421.

19. Adkins, p. 47.

20. *Ibid.*

21. *Ibid.*, p. 49.

22. *Ibid.*, p. 50.

23. *Poems of Freneau*, p. 424.

24. *Ibid.*, p. 16.

Chapter Five

1. Emerson gave up the ministry and went on the lecture platform to preach his philosophy.

2. Theodore Parker, *Theism, Atheism and The Popular Theology* (Boston, 1907), p. 304.

3. Theodore Parker, *A Discourse on The Transient and The Permanent in Christianity* (Boston 1908), p. 5.

4. "Theism, Atheism, and The Popular Theology," p. 245.

5. *Ibid.*, pp. 215, 216.

6. *Ibid.*

7. *Ibid.*, p. 155.

8. *Ibid.*, p. 301.

9. *Ibid.*, pp. 302, 303.

10. *Ibid.*, p. 293.

11. See Chap. I, p. 8., and Chap. II, p. 44.

12. "Theism, Atheism and The Popular Theology," p. 283.

13. *Ibid.*, p. 284.

14. *Ibid.*, p. 215.

15. *Ibid.*, p. 282.

16. "The Transient and The Permanent," p. 245.

17. John Weiss, *Life and Correspondence of Theodore Parker* (New York, 1864), Vol. I, p. 249.

18. "The Transient and The Permanent," p. 30.

19. *Ibid.*, p. 30.

20. "Theism, Atheism, and The Popular Theology," p. 172.

21. *Ibid.*, p. 173.

22. *Ibid.*

23. *Ibid.*, p. 182.

24. "The Transient and The Permanent," p. 22.

25. "Theism, Atheism and The Popular Theology," p. 281.

26. *Ibid.*, pp. 281, 282.

27. Theodore Parker, *Lessons in the World of Matter and the World of Man* (Chicago, 1892), p. 49.

28. "Theism, Atheism and The Popular Theology," p. 288.

29. *Ibid.*, p. 288.

30. *Ibid.*, p. 212.

31. *Ibid.*, p. 156.

32. *Ibid.*, p. 306.

33. "The Transient and The Permanent," p. 12.

34. "Theism, Atheism and The Popular Theology," p. 241.

35. *Ibid.*, p. 237.

36. *Ibid.*, p. 243.

Chapter Six

1. Van Wyck Brooks, *The Flowering of New England* (New York, 1941), p. 200.
2. *The Journals of R. W. Emerson* (Boston, 1909), Vol. I, p. 135.
3. *The Writings of R. W. Emerson* (New York, 1940), p. 106.
4. *Ibid.*, p. 115.
5. *Journals*, Vol. II, pp. 120, 121.
6. *Ibid.*, p. 419.
7. *Ibid.*, p. 424.
8. *Ibid.*, p. 487.
9. *Ibid.*, p. 490.
10. William Paley, *Natural Theology* (Boston, 1854).
11. Sherman Paul, *Emerson's Angle of Vision* (Cambridge, 1952), p. 210.
12. Perry Miller, *The Transcendentalists* (Cambridge, 1950), p. 499.
13. Brooks, *Flowering*, p. 200.
14. *Journals*, Vol. III, pp. 198, 199.
15. *Ibid.*, Vol. III, pp. 199, 200.
16. *Ibid.*, Vol. III, pp. 200, 201.
17. F. O. Mattheissen, *American Renaissance* (New York, 1941), p. 11.
18. G. H. Hartwig, "Emerson and Historical Christianity," *Hibbert Journal* (1939), Vol. XXXVII, pp. 408, 409.
19. *Journals*, Vol. III, pp. 223, 224.
20. *Ibid.*
21. P. E. Moore, "Emerson," *Cambridge History of American Literature* (New York, 1917), Vol. I, p. 357.
22. S. A. Eliot, *Heralds of A Liberal Faith* (Boston, 1910), p. 231.
23. *Journals*, Vol. I, p. 290.
24. "Lectures on the Times," *The Dial*, III (July, 1842), 13, 14, quoted in *Emerson's Angle of Vision*, Sherman Paul (Cambridge, 1952), pp. 19, 20.
25. *Ibid.*, p. 20.
26. *Ibid.*
27. *Ibid.*, p. 22.
28. *Ibid.*
29. *The Letters of Ralph Waldo Emerson*, ed. by Ralph L. Rusk (New York, 1939), Vol. I, pp. 412-13.
30. *The Writings of R. W. Emerson*, p. 20.
31. *Ibid.*, pp. 6, 7.
32. *Journals*, Vol. IV, pp. 90, 91.
33. Sherman Paul, p. 27.
34. *Ibid.*

35. *The Writings of R. W. Emerson,* p. 19.
36. *Ibid.*
37. *Ibid.*
38. *Ibid.*
39. *Ibid.,* p. 26.
40. *Ibid.,* pp. 26, 34.
41. *Ibid.,* p. 18.
42. *Ibid.,* pp. 18, 19.
43. *Ibid.,* p. 39.
44. *Ibid.*
45. *Ibid.,* p. 80.
46. *Ibid.,* p. 73.
47. *Ibid.,* pp. 74, 75.
48. *Ibid.,* p. 80.
49. *Ibid.,* pp. 80, 81.
50. *Ibid.,* p. 81.
51. Perry Miller, p. 211.
52. *Ibid.,* pp. 210, 211.
53. *Ibid.,* pp. 212, 213.
54. *The Writings of R. W. Emerson,* p. 72.
55. *Young Emerson Speaks,* ed. Arthure C. McGiffert (Boston, 1938), p. 122.
56. *Journals,* Vol. II, p. 409.
57. G. H. Hartwig, p. 410.
58. *Ibid.*
59. See Chap. I.
60. G. H. Hartwig, p. 411.
61. Arthur Christy, *The Orient in American Transcendentalism* (New York, 1932), p. 11.
62. *The Writings of R. W. Emerson,* p. 185.
63. *Journals,* Vol. II, p. 180.
64. F. I. Carpenter, *Emerson Handbook* (New York, 1953), p. 145.
65. *Ibid.,* p. 147.
66. *The Writings of R. W. Emerson,* p. 69.
67. F. I. Carpenter, p. 146.
68. *Journals,* Vol. I, pp. 96, 97.
69. *Ibid.,* Vol. III, p. 423.
70. P. H. Boynton, "Emerson In His Period," *International Journal of Ethics,* Vol. XXXIX (1929), p. 180.
71. *The Writings of R. W. Emerson,* p. 175.
72. *Ibid.,* p. 276.
73. Arthur Christy, p. 81.
74. *Ibid.,* p. 80.
75. *Ibid.*
76. *The Writings of R. W. Emerson,* p. 264.

77. *Ibid.*, p. 277.
78. Quoted by Christy, p. 84.
79. *The Bhagavadgita*, ed. S. Radhakrishnan (New York, 1948), pp. 307, 313.
80. *The Writings of R. W. Emerson*, p. 262.
81. *Ibid.*, p. 266.
82. *Ibid.*, p. 36.
83. *Ibid.*, p. 277.
84. *The Writings of R. W. Emerson*, p. 289.
85. *Ibid.*, p. 287.
86. *Ibid.*, p. 289.
87. *Ibid.*, p. 84.

Chapter Seven

1. G. W. Allen, *The Solitary Singer* (New York, 1955), pp. 156, 462.
2. William James, *The Varieties of Religious Experience* (New York, 1902), p. 87.
3. *Ibid.*, p. 99.
4. Walt Whitman, *Leaves of Grass and Selected Prose,* Rinehart Edition (New York, 1949), p. 25.
5. F. O. Matthiessen, *American Renaissance* (New York, 1941), p. 11.
6. "Democratic Vistas," quoted in *Leaves of Grass and Selected Prose* (New York, 1949), p. 521.
7. Allen, *Singer*, p. 242.
7ᵃ. Emory Holloway, *Walt Whitman: Complete Poetry and Selected Prose and Letters,* (London, 1938), pp. 1045, 1046.
8. R. W. Emerson, *Selected Writings* (New York, 1940), p. 36.
9. Walt Whitman, *Leaves of Grass and Selected Prose* (New York, 1949), p. 43.
10. Emerson, *Selected Writings*, p. 435.
11. "Song of Myself," p. 45.
12. Emerson, *Selected Writings*, p. 294.
13. "Song of the Open Road," p. 127.
14. *Ibid.*
15. "Song of Myself," p. 75.
16. G. W. Allen, *Walt Whitman Handbook* (New York, 1946), pp. 255, 256.
17. *Ibid.*, p. 257.
18. *Ibid.*
19. Allen, *Handbook*, pp. 257, 258.
20. *Ibid.*
21. See Chap. V.
22. Emerson, *Selected Writings*, p. 36.

23. R. W. Emerson, *Nature*, pp. 40, 41.
24. "Song of Myself," p. 27.
25. *Ibid.*, pp. 56, 58.
26. Quoted in David Daiches, *Walt Whitman, Man, Poet, Philosopher*. Three Lectures Presented Under the Auspices of the Gertrude Clarke Whittall Poetry and Literature Fund, Washington, The Library of Congress, 1955, p. 48.
27. "One's-Self I Sing," p. 1.
28. David Daiches, p. 37.
29. "Sleepers," p. 351.
30. "To Think of Time," p. 363.
31. G. W. Allen, *Handbook*, p. 264.
32. *Ibid.*
33. "Song of Myself," p. 71.
34. "Calamus," p. 98.
35. Allen, *Handbook*, p. 267.
36. "Song of Myself," p. 29.
37. "Calamus," p. 98.
38. "Song of Myself," p. 40 ff.
39. Allen, *Handbook*, p. 268.
40. "Song of Myself," p. 50.
41. *Ibid.*, p. 51.
42. *Ibid.*, p. 69.
43. *Ibid.*
44. *Ibid.*, pp. 69, 70.
45. Allen, *Handbook*, p. 269.
46. "Ages and Ages Returning at Intervals," p. 93.
47. "Children of Adam," pp. 80, 86.
48. *Ibid.*, p. 91.
49. *Ibid.*, pp. 89, 91.
50. "Song of Myself," p. 23.
51. "I Sit and Look Out," pp. 229, 230.
52. Allen, *Handbook*, p. 265.
53. "The Sleepers," p, 356.
54. "Faces," pp. 380, 382.
55. Allen, *Handbook*, p. 266.
56. "Song of Myself," p. 42.
57. "Starting From Paumanok," p. 15.
58. "Crossing Brooklyn Ferry," p. 136.
59. Allen, *Handbook*, p. 273.
60. *Ibid.*
61. Allen, *Handbook*, p. 274.
62. S. Radhakrishnan, *The Bhagavadgita*, pp. 70, 71.
63. Allen, *Handbook*, p. 275.
64. "Song of Prudence," p. 311.

65. *Ibid.*, p. 313.
66. *Ibid.*, p. 311.
67. *Ibid.*, p. 312.
68. *Ibid.*, p. 312.
69. Allen, *Handbook*, p. 276.
70. Emerson, *Selected Writings*, p. 175.
71. *Ibid.*, p. 245.
72. "Song of Myself," pp. 24, 25.
73. *The Uncollected Poetry and Prose of Walt Whitman*, ed. Emory Holloway (New York, 1932), Vol. II, p. 74.
74. "Thou Mother with Thy Equal Brood," p. 376.
75. "As I Lay With My Head in Your Lap Comerado," p. 268.
76. "Song of Myself," p. 41.
77. "Song of Myself," p. 65.
78. "Miracles," p. 323.
79. Allen, *Handbook*, p. 270.
80. *Ibid.*
81. "Starting from Paumanok," p. 15.
82. "Song of Myself," p. 71.
83. *Ibid.*, p. 49.
84. "Song of The Open Road," p. 131.
85. "Thou Mother With Thy Equal Brood," p. 374.
86. "Song of Myself," p. 25.
87. "Song of Myself," p. 64.
88. *Ibid.*, pp. 67, 68.
89. G. L. Sixbey, "Chanting The Square Deific," *American Literature*, IX (May, 1937), p. 174.
90. *Ibid.*, p. 179.
91. *Ibid.*, p. 180.
92. *Ibid.*, p. 184.
93. "Chanting the Square Deific," p. 365.
94. *Ibid.*, p. 366.
95. Sixbey, p. 186.
96. Sixbey, p. 190.
97. *Ibid.*, p. 190.
98. *Ibid.*, p. 193.
99. "Chanting The Square Deific," p. 366.
100. G. W. Allen, *Handbook*, p. 303.
101. "Democratic Vistas," p. 521.
102. Allen, *Handbook*, p. 305.
103. *Ibid.*, p. 306.
104. *Ibid.*, p. 307.
105. *Ibid.*, p. 308.
106. *Ibid.*

107. See Norton's attack on Emerson's *Divinity School Address,* Chap. VI.

108. Allen, *Handbook,* p. 310.

109. *Ibid.,* p. 310.

110. *Ibid.,* pp. 310, 311.

111. *Ibid.*

112. *Ibid.*

113. *Ibid.,* p. 311.

114. "One's-Self I Sing," p. 1.

115. "Democratic Vistas," pp. 500, 501.

116. "By Blue Ontario's Shores," p. 283.

117. "Democratic Vistas," p. 504.

118. Preface to 1855 Edition, *Leaves of Grass,* pp. 470, 471.

119. "Democratic Vistas," p. 507.

120. *Ibid.,* p. 507.

121. "For You, O Democracy," p. 100.

122. "Salut Au Monde," p. 123.

123. *The Writings of R. W. Emerson,* p. 433.

124. "Thou Mother with Thy Equal Brood," p. 373.

125. "Song of the Redwood Tree," pp. 175, 176.

126. *Ibid.,* p. 177.

127. "The Sleepers," p. 356.

128. "Passage to India," p. 341.

Epilogue

1. O. W. Holmes, *Mechanism In Thoughts and Morals* (Cambridge, 1892), p. 305.

2. *Ibid.,* p. 310.

3. Frank Norris, *The Octopus* (New York, 1957), p. 86.

4. *Ibid.,* p. 310.

5. Quoted in F. I. Carpenter, *American Literature and The Dream* (New York, 1955), p. 169.

6. *Ibid.,* p. 168.

7. Walter Van Tilburg Clark, *The Ox-Bow Incident* (New York, 1940), p. 67.

8. Wallace Stevens, *Selected Poems* (New York, 1959), p. 7.

Bibliography

PRIMARY REFERENCES

ADKINS, NELSON, F. *Philip Freneau and The Cosmic Enigma.* New York University Press, 1949.

ALLEN, ETHAN. *Reason, The Only Oracle of Man.* New York, 1836.

ALLEN, G. W. *Walt Whitman Handbook.* New York, 1947.

ALLEN, G. W. *The Solitary Singer.* New York, 1955.

BOYNTON, P. H. "Emerson In His Period," *International Journal of Ethics,* XXXLX (Jan., 1929), 177-89.

BROOKS, VAN WYCK. *The Flowering of New England, 1815-1865.* Revised Edition, New York, 1941.

BROOKS, VAN WYCK. *The Life of Emerson.* New York, 1932.

CARPENTER, F. I. *American Literature and The Dream.* New York, 1955.

CARPENTER, F. I. *Emerson Handbook.* New York, 1953.

CHRISTY, ARTHUR. *The Orient in American Transcendentalism.* New York, 1932.

CLARK, WALTER VAN TILBURG. *The Ox-Bow Incident.* New York, 1940.

DAICHES, DAVID. *Walt Whitman, Man, Poet, Philosopher.* The Library of Congress, 1955.

DAVIES, A. POWELL. *The First Christian: A Study of St. Paul and Christian Origins.* Mentor Books, 1957.

DEWEY, JOHN. *The Living Thoughts of Jefferson.* New York, 1940.

EMERSON, RALPH WALDO. *The Journals.* 10 vols., Boston, 1909.

EMERSON, RALPH WALDO. *The Letters.* New York, 1939.

EMERSON, RALPH WALDO. *The Selected Writings.* New York, 1940.

ELIOT, S. A. *Heralds of a Liberal Faith.* 3 vols., Boston, 1910.

FRAZER, JAMES G. *The New Golden Bough.* Revised and edited by T. H. Gaster. New York, 1959.

FRENEAU, PHILIP. *Poems of Freneau.* New York, 1929.

HARTWIG, G. H. "Emerson and Historical Christianity," *Hibbert Journal,* XXXVII (1939), 405-12.

HOLLOWAY, EMORY. *The Uncollected Poetry and Prose of Walt Whitman.* 2 vols., New York, 1932.

HOLLOWAY, EMORY. *Walt Whitman: Complete Poetry and Selected Prose and Letters,* London, 1938.

HOLMES, O. W. *Mechanism In Thought and Morals.* Cambridge, 1892.

JAMES, WILLIAM. *The Varieties of Religious Experience.* New York, 1902.

JEFFERSON, THOMAS. *The Life and Selected Writings.* New York, 1944.

LEARY, LEWIS. *That Rascal Freneau.* Rutgers University Press, 1941.

LEHMANN, KARL. *Thomas Jefferson, American Humanist.* New York, 1947.

MATHER, COTTON. *The Christian Philosopher.* London, 1721. University Microfilms, American Culture Series.

MATTHIESSEN, F. O. *American Renaissance.* New York, 1941.

McGIFFERT, ARTHUR C. *Young Emerson Speaks.* Boston, 1938.

MILLER, PERRY. *The Transcendentalists.* Harvard University Press, 1950.

MOORE, CECIL A. *English Prose of the Eighteenth Century.* New York, 1933.

MOORE, P. E. "Emerson," *Cambridge History of American Literature.* New York, 1933.

MORAIS, HERBERT M. *Deism in Eighteenth Century America.* New York, 1934.

NORRIS, FRANK. *The Octopus.* New York, 1957.

PAINE, THOMAS. *The Age of Reason.* Baltimore, n.d.

PALEY, WILLIAM. *Natural Theology.* Boston, 1854.

PARKER, THEODORE. *A Discourse on the Transient and the Permanent in Christianity.* Boston, 1908.

PARKER, THEODORE. *Collected Works.* 15 vols., Boston, 1907.

PARKER, THEODORE. *Lessons From The World of Matter and The World of Man.* Chicago, 1892.

PAUL, SHERMAN. *Emerson's Angle of Vision.* Harvard University Press, 1952.

RADHAKRISHNAN, S. *The Bhagavadgita.* New York, 1948.

SIXBEY, G. L. "Chanting The Square Deific," *American Literature,* IX, (May, 1937), 171-95.

STUART, RANDALL. *American Literature and Christian Doctrine.* Louisiana State University, 1958.

STEINBECK, JOHN. *To A God Unknown.* New York, 1933.

STEINBECK, JOHN. *The Grapes of Wrath.* New York, 1939.

STEVENS, WALLACE. *Selected Poems.* New York, 1959.

WEISS, JOHN. *Life and Correspondence of Theodore Parker.* 2 vols., New York, 1864.

WHITMAN, WALT. *Leaves of Grass and Selected Prose,* edited by Sculley Bradley. Rinehart Editions, New York, 1949.

WILLEY, BASIL. *The Seventeenth Century Background.* New York, 1953.

SECONDARY REFERENCES

ALBRIGHT, W. F. *From the Stone Age to Christianity.* Second Edition, New York, 1957.

BARNES, H. E. *The Twilight of Christianity.* New York, 1929.

BUTLER, JOSEPH. *The Analogy of Religion, Natural and Revealed To the Constitution and Course of Nature.* 10th Edition, New York, 1841.

CHADBOURNE, P. A. *Lectures On Natural Theology.* New York, 1867.

CHINARD, G. *Thomas Jefferson, The Apostle of Americanism.* Boston, 1929.

COMMAGER, H. S. "Tempest in Boston Tea Cup," *New England Quarterly,* VI (Dec., 1933), 651-75.

CONNER, F. W. *Cosmic Optimism.* University of Florida Press, 1949.

COOKE, G. W. *Unitarianism in America.* Boston, 1902.

DAS, BHAGAVAN. *The Essential Unity of all Religions.* 3rd Edition, Benares, 1947.

DAWSON, J. W. *Nature and the Bible.* New York, 1875.

EDDINGTON, ARTHUR STANLEY. *Science and the Unseen World.* New York, 1929.

EMERTON, E. *Unitarian Thought.* New York, 1911.

Encyclopaedia Brittanica. 14th Edition, "Bible," 1954.

FLINT, ROBERT. *Anti-Theistic Theories.* London, 1879.

FISKE, JOHN. *Through Nature To God.* Boston, 1899.

FOERSTER, NORMAN. *Nature In American Literature.* New York, 1923.

FROTHINGHAM, O. B. *Boston Unitarianism.* New York, 1890.

GOHDES, C. L. F. *The Periodicals of American Transcendentalism.* Duke University Press, 1931.

HARRIS, E. E. *Revelation Through Reason.* New Haven, 1958.

HOLBROOK, STEWARD, H. *Ethan Allen.* New York, 1940.

HUME, DAVID. *Dialogues Concerning Natural Religion.* Oxford, 1935.

HUXLEY, JULIAN. *Religion Without Revelation.* London, 1957.

INGE, W. R. *The Philosophy of Plotinus.* London, 1923.

JOYCE, G. H. *Principles of Natural Theology.* New York, 1934.

KOCH, G. A. *Republican Religion.* New York, 1933.

LANE, H. H. *Evolution and Christian Faith.* Princeton University Press, 1923.

LEWIS, R. W. B. *The American Adam.* University of Chicago Press, 1955.

MULLER, F. M. *Anthropological Religion,* New York, 1903.

PARKER, THEODORE. *Experience as a Minister.* Boston, 1859.

RENAN, ERNEST. *Life of Jesus.* Boston, 1895.

RILEY, I. W. *American Philosophy: The Early Schools.* New York, 1907.

SEELEY, J. R. *Natural Religion.* London, 1882.

SIMPSON, J. Y. *The Spiritual Interpretation of Nature.* London, 1925.

SMITH, F. M. "Whitman's Poet-Prophet and Carlyle's Hero," *PMLA,* LV (Dec., 1940), 1146-64.

SPECTOR, R. D. *Deism In The Writings of Theodore Parker.* M.A. Thesis, New York University, 1949.

STEPHENS, LESLIE. *History of English Thought in the Eighteenth Century.* 2 vols., London, 1902.

TEMPLE, WILLIAM. *Nature, Man and God.* London, 1935.

TYNDALL, C. H. *Through Science To God; Nature a Medium In The Revelation of Spiritual Truth.* New York, 1926.

WALCUTT, C. *American Naturalism: A Divided Stream.* University of Missouri Press, 1956.

WHITEHEAD, A. N. *Science and The Modern World.* New York, 1925.

WILLEY, BASIL. *The Religion of Nature.* London, 1957.

Index